Circus Days
in
Sarasota and Venice

Kim Cool

Kim Dael

Circus Days

in
Sarasota and Venice

By

Kim Cool

HISTORIC VENICE PRESS

Also by Kim Cool:
Ghost Stories of Venice
Ghost Stories of Sarasota

Circus Days in Sarasota and Venice

© 2004 Kim Cool

Historic Venice Press
P. O. Box 800, Venice, FL 34284
941.468-6556
kimcool@www.historicvenicepress.com

First Edition April 2004
Printed in the United States of America
ISBN   0-9721655-3-3

To the circus performers and friends
who shared their memories
of a special time
in the history of the
cities of Sarasota and Venice,
a time that is gone
but hopefully,
will not be forgotten.

Original painting by Beverly Fleming
Color prints are available at the Beverly Fleming Gallery in Sarasota and at the gift shop of the John & Mable Ringling Museum of Art.

Contents

Kim Cool

The Museum of the Circus at the John and Mable
Ringling Museum of Art in Sarasota, Fla. contains a
wealth of information about all the circuses that have
called Sarasota County home, including The Greatest
Show on Earth, which wintered in Sarasota and Venice for
more than 64 years.

Sarasota County was the winter destination of The Greatest Show on Earth, the Ringling Bros. and Barnum & Bailey Circus, for more years than any other place on earth — a total of 65 years.

Before the Ringling show's foray into the south, the giant traveling circus had wintered first where it began, in Baraboo, Wisconsin, from 1884 to 1918. With the merger of the Ringling and Barnum shows, the circus moved to Bridgeport, Conn., staying there until 1927.

Overnight, tents replaced tarpon as the primary lure for northern sunseekers during the winter months.

Immersing himself in the business, social and cultural life of the still young city, the show's owner, John Ringling, had commissioned the construction of Ca d'Zan (house of John) on his 20-acre parcel three years earlier, in 1924. That year he also was making plans to build a Ritz-Carlton Hotel on Longboat Key and to build the John & Mable Ringling Museum of Art.

He would have brought the circus to Sarasota sooner but his brother Charles, who lived on an adjacent piece of property along Sarasota Bay, continually vetoed that plan.

Following Charles' death in 1926, John Ringling finally got his way. During the winter of 1927-28, John

Ringling brought his circus to the site of the old fair-grounds in Sarasota.

It was a move that forever changed the destiny of Sarasota County and the cities of Sarasota and Venice.

Circus performers from all over the world soon settled in the area, adding to the area's culture and to its cultural diversity.

The circus became as big a draw to tourists as the sugar-sand beaches of Siesta Key or the prehistoric sharks teeth found on the beaches of Venice. Tourism flourished. Ringling's museum was soon accompanied by an art school and, despite the entrepreneur's death in 1936, the area's extraordinary future was secure.

The two cities would become known as cultural hubs, cities in which the average resident had a strong affinity for the arts.

Sarasota, the larger city, boasts an opera house, several theater companies, a symphony, art and historical associations and a world-renowned botanical garden.

Venice, despite a population of just 20,000, has its own art center, nationally known community theater, symphony, concert band and opera guild, plus countless clubs and organizations related to art and culture. It is a MainStreet City, proud of its history and its legacy as a John Nolen-planned community.

Although the Ringling circus departed Venice in

1992, it could not begin to take everything that it had brought to the city. It left more than memories and a way of life behind. Still making their homes in Venice are a number of circus greats and near-greats. Some were performers. Others were managers or concession-aires or seamstresses. They were part of The Greatest Show on Earth and they remain a part of Venice.

Many of those people shared their memories with me as I set out to tell the story of the most colorful years in the history of the Cultural Coast, the 65 years when the Ringling Bros. Barnum & Bailey Circus came home to Sarasota and to Venice.

The tents are gone and as this book was being shipped off to the printer, plans were being made to tear down the old arena and replace it with an industrial park, but memo-ries linger. There are plenty of those in these two cities.

In homage to John Ringling, each chapter title in this book is embellished with a photo of the late showman as a clown. The photo is from the collection of circus histo-rian Bob Horne who contributed a great deal to this book. It is thought to be one of very few remaining photos of Ringling as a clown, taken when he was 18 or 19 years old.

That the area encompassing Sarasota and Venice is today known as the Cultural Coast can be directly attrib-uted to Ringling, his museum and even his circus.

The roots of that nickname can be traced directly to

Ringling's arrival in Sarasota and his decision to build his museum to attract that type of person to the city. Established about the same time was the Players Theatre, which was quickly followed by the Asolo Theatre Company, the opera, ballet, art league and similar cultural institutions. Ringling himself hastened the cultural explosion by establishing the Ringling School of Art shortly after his museum opened.

Several circuses continue to winter in the area but the biggest one of them all is gone, possibly forever. Only a plaque remains to mark the Sarasota site and it is but a matter of time before the old Venice circus arena will be demolished to make way for something else.

Were it not for the cultural vision of Ringling, the fortunes of these two cities might have been very different.

After all, this area was home to the greatest circus names in history: Animal trainer Gunther Gebel-Williams, clowns such as Emmett Kelly, Lou Jacobs and Frosty Little, wire walkers such as the Great Wallendas, the Cristianis, the Concellos, circus band leader Merle Evans, and performers LaNorma, Unus, the Zacchinis, Dime Wilson, aerialist Tito Gaona and so many more.

Some say they can still hear the sound of the animals.

Is it the roar of the surf or the roar of the crowds?

"Ladies and gentlemen, children of all ages ... the circus!"

Part One

Circus Days in Sarasota

Photo courtesy of Bob Horne

Sarasota winter quarters of the Ringling Bros. and Barnum & Bailey Circus in 1954. The property had room for four complete trains, a tent-making shop, wagon repair shop, offices, menagerie, dormitories for performers, commissary and a variety of rehearsal areas, most of which were open to the public in those years. Big changes were just five years away.

Sarasota: a 3-ring town

On Christmas Day, 1927, the city of Sarasota received what many would consider its all-time greatest Christmas gift — the circus.

Wrapped in the same colorful package was the city's destiny as the cultural capital of the state of Florida.

The gift was bestowed by John Ringling, the real estate tycoon who built the John & Mable Ringling Museum of Art to lure wealthy property buyers away from the east coast of Florida to Sarasota.

Ringling also just happened to be the owner of The Greatest Show on Earth.

For 34 years that show wintered at Ringlingville, in Baraboo, Wisconsin, before moving to Bridgeport, Conn., where it spent its final decade in the north after

The two postcards pictured above and below are from the personal collection of Larry Kellogg, who works as a publicist for the Ringling Bros. and Barnum & Bailey Circus in the greater Tampa/St. Petersburg area. The bottom card depicts the Sarasota winter quarters in its early days.

combining with the old Barnum & Bailey show. The biggest flock of snowbirds ever was about to descend on Sarasota.

The Ringling Bros. and Barnum & Bailey Circus was heading south for the winter, the first circus to do so. It would not be the last.

Ringling made the announcement March 23, 1927, just before the circus opened its 1927 season at Madison Square Garden in New York City.

This was a financial windfall for the city of Sarasota, one that would have a positive economic impact on the city and mold its destiny far into the future. For even when the circus leaves town, much of the magic

Main Entrance,
Ringling Bros. and Barnum & Bailey Winter Quarters

Postcard courtesy of Larry Kellogg

The entrance to the Sarasota winter quarters of the Ringling Bros. and Barnum & Bailey Circus, in the late 1920s shortly after its opening.

remains. That is as true in Baraboo as in Sarasota and Venice — three towns where the circus was in residence for at least 30 years and where far more than memories still remain.

Though the circus has been gone from Baraboo for nearly a century, that city still is famous as the original home of the Ringling circus, which had developed there because John Ringling's father, August, had established a harness-making business at Baraboo in the mid-1870s. It was a natural choice when August's five sons established their circus in 1884.

Since the founding of the Circus World Museum in that city in 1959, and the naming of nine historic land-

GIRAFFES AT RINGLING BROS. WINTER QUARTERS, SARASOTA, FLA.   110

Postcard courtesy of Larry Kellogg

Giraffes were but a small part of the huge circus menagerie in its early days in Sarasota.

mark circus structures dating to the years 1897-1916, people have flocked to Baraboo to visit these sites and to learn about the history of the circus.

They also come to Sarasota.

Ringling's timing was perfect for Sarasota. Florida's real estate boom was coming to a screeching halt and the Great Depression was looming just ahead. This influx of people with jobs and money would save the city and allow its growth to continue nearly unabated. It may even have saved Ringling himself from bankruptcy.

The circus would spend approximately $500,000 for buildings on the new site. The city and the city council, with help from some wealthy developers, including A. B. Edwards, Ralph Caples and A. E. Cummer, would ante up the land in a special lease deal. Two railroads, the Atlantic Coast Line and the Seaboard Air Line Railroad brought spur lines to the site.

What famous circus performer Jennie Wallenda would describe as "the greatest winter quarters" for the Greatest Show officially opened Dec. 25.

"We never lived in Venice," she said. "The Sarasota quarters had everything."There were 50 elephants, 500 horses, lions and tigers. and the trains were parked there too. When "The Greatest Show on Earth" was filmed, it was filmed there."

Race, religion and national origin mattered not in the

global village of the circus. The Ringling show sought the best performers in each area of the show. It did not matter where they had been born. John Ringling sought out the best, period. His successors have continued to do the same. The list of circus stars that have been signed to perform in The Greatest Show on Earth includes Lillian Leitzel, a Hungarian star on the Roman rings; the wire-walking Wallendas and, years later, the famed animal trainer Gunther Gebel-Williams, from Germany; the Cristiani riding family from Italy; Asian acrobats, the Naittos Troupe; Australian equestrian May Worth; Mexican trapeze artist Alfredo Codono; and Tito Gaona, who today runs a school for aerialists in Venice.

Ringling was at the peak of his career when he brought the circus to Sarasota; he had been considered one of the wealthiest men in America in 1925. He was happily married to the love of his life, Mable Burton Ringling. Together they were overseeing the construction of their dream house, Ca d'Zan, and spending thousands of dollars on its furnishings as well as on their art collection. They were well-traveled and closely associated with some of the biggest names in show business, names like Flo Ziegfeld and Billie Burke.

When they traveled in the United States, it often was aboard the JoMar, the private rail car built for John in

1917 and named for John and Mable. Ringling also had a spur track built out into Sarasota Bay, where the car was kept when in Sarasota.

"There were no mosquitoes there," circus historian Bob Horne said. "It wasn't stinky either."

The bay location solved the nasty problem of what to do with waste from the train car in an era before pump out stations. Deluxe in every way, the custom train car had two bathtubs, at least three toilets, a galley,

Photo by Kim Cool

Bob Horne and several other Sarasota businessmen are working to restore the JoMar, the private train car built in 1917 for John Ringling.

three bedrooms, living room, dining room, galley and crew quarters. It did not have holding tanks for waste water of any kind. Whatever went into the toilets or down the sink drain was eliminated on the track below. When parked in one spot for a time, this could be a smelly problem. The bay provided the perfect solution

Photo by Kim Cool

Bob Horne points out John Ringling's custom-made narrow bathtub aboard the JoMar, Ringling's private train car.

for the time.

Nor did the deluxe car have air conditioning. The bay location must have been cooler as well.

What the car did have was concrete floors covered with rubber tile, the latest thing in 1917. Now curly and somewhat dried out, most of the tile flooring still remains. Horne said the tiles will be removed, refreshed and sold to offset the costs of restoring the train car.

The JoMar also had real brass beds, Mexican mahogany wood sills and steel cabinets, closets and doors painted with faux wood finishing techniques to match the real wood.

There was a buzzer system to summon the steward, and a formal dining room with fine linens and silver. Horne said one of the original linen table settings is in the hands of a private owner who has promised to give it to him for display when the car's restoration is complete.

Restoration may take awhile as the years have not been kind to the car. It was remodeled and used by John Ringling North until Feld Entertainment bought the circus but then, because it was owned by the Ringling family and was not part of the circus sale, it sat unused on a siding near the Venice Train Depot from 1971 to 1985. North had paid to have it taken there after getting a call from Rudy Bundy, a former Ringling chairman and father-in-law of Bob Horne.

Bundy had his own band and occasionally would sit in, playing clarinet, with the Merle Evans-directed circus band.

Merle Evans' contract was signed aboard the JoMar, Horne said. In addition to the circus greats who might have been invited aboard the all-steel, 81-foot, 11-inch long rail car, Ringling wined and dined the rich and

Photo by Kim Cool

Bob Horne in the dining room of the JoMar, Ringling's private train car. Drawers are missing but the cabinet is basically intact, although in need of fresh paint. A donor has already promised a painting that once hung on the opposite wall. Restoration work is under way in Sarasota.

Photo courtesy of Bob Horne

When the JoMar was brand new in 1917, the dining room looked like this. Notice the fan. There was no air conditioning in those days. Leaded glass windows will be replicated by a local artist for the restored car.

famous of his day, from Tom Mix to General John Joseph Pershing, a guest during World War I. While on board for the night in 1932, Mix put $100,000 in a safe beneath his bed, Horne said. The next morning his valet and the $100,000 were gone, never to be seen again.

Next to the JoMar on the Venice siding was the RB 66 (RB stands for Rudy Bundy) Horne spent his honeymoon aboard the RB 66 in 1971 and so did several members of his family in the ensuing years.

Horne has wanted to restore the JoMar since the 1980s and even went so far as to have it primed in 1984.

In 1985 the two cars were taken to a rail museum in Indiana as part of a package deal, but the JoMar was not wanted there and was brought back to Sarasota County in 1990 by the JoMar Society, Horne said.

"For 24 years that 88-ton railroad car has been a millstone around my neck," he said. "This is its last chance. She is at that cusp. She will either be saved or scrapped."

Although the Railroad Museum in Parrish estimated it would cost $450,000 to restore the car, Horne was convinced that, with donated materials and lots of volunteer hours, he could do the job for under $100,000. As this book went to press, the JoMar was on a donated siding in Sarasota, off School Avenue and Fruitville Road, where it was expected to become part of a five-

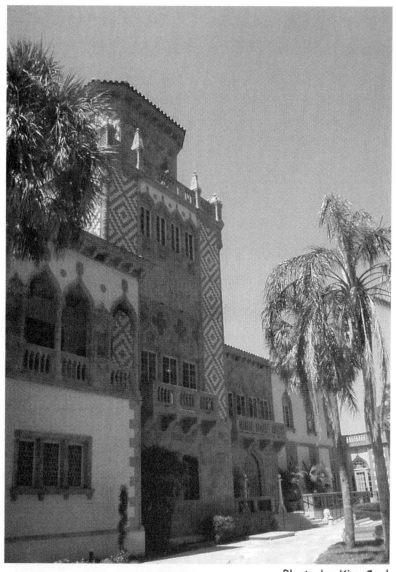

Photo by Kim Cool

Ca d'Zan, the winter home of John and Mable Ringling. Completed in 1927 at a cost of $1.5 million, the home's restoration cost in excess of $15 million in 2002.

Kim Cool

Photos courtesy of Linda Fagan
One of the most famous circus bandleaders was Merle Evans, who signed his contract on board the JoMar.

The little girl in the center bottom of the picture is Linda Fagan when she was 5. She is holding a bucket. The painting was from Fagan's late parents' home.

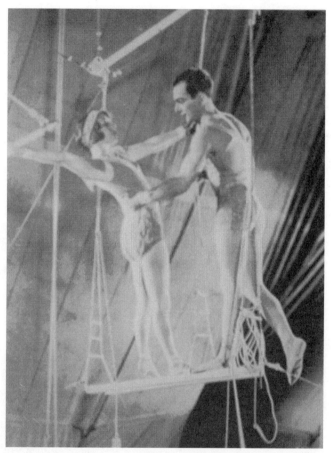

Photo courtesy of Linda Fagan
The Cristianis rehearse their aerial act in a tent that is believed to be the Ringling show tent at Sarasota Winter Quarters, circa 1950.

theater arts enclave, which will include the Jomar and possibly four additional restored train cars, Horne said.

I climbed aboard the Jomar in late January 2004, carefully watching my every step lest I fall through a hole in the floor. Despite its condition, I could see, like Horne, what it could become and was hopeful that the historic train car would be saved.

Fortunately, Ca d'Zan, the Ringling mansion, never was in such disrepair yet it too needed much work to be restored to its former glory. The project took nearly six

Photo by Kim Cool

The former home of Charles Ringling is now used as an administrative building for New College, a liberal arts college that is part of the University of South Florida in Sarasota.

years and an expenditure of some $15 million by the time it was completed in 2002.

The Ringlings entertained at their first party at Ca d'Zan on Christmas Day 1926, shortly after the death of John's brother Charles, who lived just to the north in his own Italian-inspired mansion. It was one year, nearly to the day, before the circus moved into its then-new Sarasota winter quarters, brought there by the last surviving Ringling brother, John.

The Ringling home had cost $1.5 million to build, roughly one year's revenue of the circus in those days. Maintaining the Jomar cost approximately $100,000 per year, including the payroll for its steward and chef.

Despite the onset of the Great Depression, the circus continued to bring in more than $1 million a year in the 1930s.

Photo courtesy of Bob Horne
There were six rail sidings for the 100 train cars stored at Ringling Circus winter quarters complex in Sarasota. Two different rail lines ran alongside the 200-acre site.

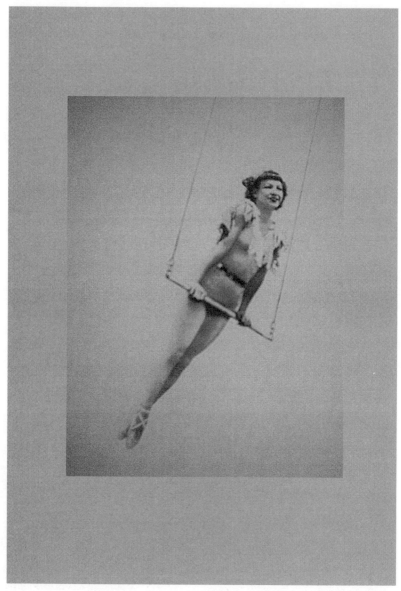

Photo courtesy of Linda Fagan

Annette Concello was the first wife of Art Concello and part of the team, the Flying Concellos.

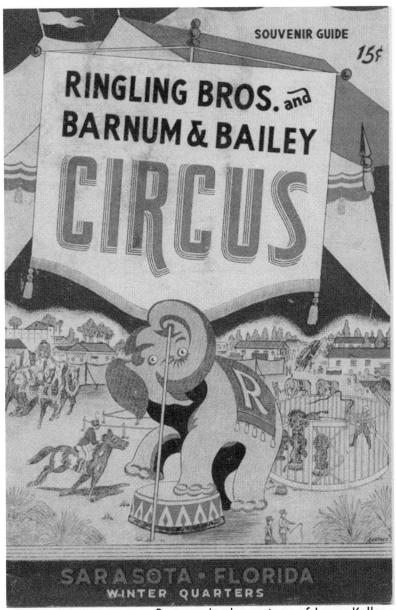

Program book courtesy of Larry Kellogg

Visitors to the Sarasota winter quarters in 1937 could purchase these souvenir program books for 15 cents each.

21

Radio, film and even the automobile would begin to affect that income stream during the next three decades.

A 1926 hurricane had left a serious mark on the city and by 1927, when the circus arrived in the city, investor interest in Florida began to weaken. The stock market began to sputter. Yet Ringling pressed on, beginning construction of his art museum that same year.

Remaining optimistic despite losing the financing for his dream hotel, a Ritz-Carlton for Sarasota, he pledged both personal and circus assets against an increasing pile of debts. Neither Mable's death from Addison's Disease in June 1929 nor the onset of the Great Depression deterred him. When he lost the contract for his circus to perform at Madison Square Garden because the Sells-Floto Circus had been booked there, he simply borrowed an additional $1.7 million to buy out his competitor's parent company, the American Circus Corp., and regained his place at the Garden. With the purchase of the American Circus Corp., Ringling became owner of all the major circus railroad shows in the United States: Hagenbeck-Wallace Circus, John Robinson Circus, Sparks Circus, A. G. Barnes Circus and the Sells-Floto Circus. Ringling finessed the most stupendous circus deal in history. (He kept those circuses on the road. Only when they lost money did he close them down, yet con-

Photos courtesy of Linda Fagan

Another view, circa the late 1940s, of the Sarasota Winter Quarters of The Greatest Show on Earth. The photo below hangs on Linda Fagan's wall. From left, Pat Valdo, John Ringling North and Art Concello, the man who would save the show.

tinuing to hold the title to their various names. The Hagenbach and Wallace name was reused to identify the company that makes costumes and props for The Greatest Show on Earth.

John even borrowed $50,000 from his second wife, Emily Buck, shortly before the end of their disastrous marriage. As his problems became public, Mable's sisters joined what would become a lengthy line of litigants in search of a piece of Ringling's assets.

The museum opened on schedule in 1932 but control of that and the circus had been taken from him. It would be run by trustees, with Sam Gumpertz named

Postcard courtesy of Larry Kellogg

Clowns Lou Jacobs and Emmett Kelly play with an elephant and its rider during an outdoor rehearsal at the Sarasota winter quarters of The Greatest Show on Earth in 1947.

as the general manager of the show. In failing health and just four years before his death, the once wealthy tycoon had become dependent on the parking revenue from the museum. He had even been locked out of his New York apartment. He owed $3.25 for his newspaper subscription and $13 million to the Internal Revenue Service, but somehow he and his advisors had managed to safeguard the key to Sarasota's future — the art museum and its collection.

Suffering from a string of blood clots to his brain, and confined to a wheelchair, Ringling divorced Emily in 1933.

Just days before his house would have been seized and sold to satisfy debts, Ringling died. It was Dec. 2, 1936. His nephew John Ringling North became the director of the circus two years later. Like his famous uncle, he too would have to struggle to save the show near the end of his reign. But first, there were problems that did not die with John.

The advent of World War II added to the problems already growing within the circus.

North scaled back the show from a six-pole big top to a four-pole tent but with so many men off to fight the war, even that was tough to erect.

The Office of Defense Transportation dictated the train schedule, adding to the show's scheduling problems. These problems paled against two events that might have put the giant show out of business altogether.

While playing Cleveland, Ohio, on August 4, 1942, disaster struck The Greatest Show on Earth. The skies were clear and the circus audience were about to experience a first — an air-conditioned tent.

While Clevelanders were making their way to the circus lot next to the Cleveland Municipal Stadium on the shores of Lake Erie, performers were gathering for lunch at the cookhouse. The animals in the menagerie were grazing away when, all of a sudden, someone yelled "fire!"

While lake breezes fanned and fed the flames, all hands tried to douse the fire and move animals to safety. Almost as quickly as the fire had started, it ended, but not before taking a toll. Dead were four elephants, 13 camels, every zebra in the show, five lions, two tigers, two giraffes, two deer, two donkeys, a puma, a chimpanzee, one ostrich and an axis deer, a loss of some $200,000, according to North.

Miraculously, the air-conditioned performance tent was saved and the evening show went on as scheduled.

Adding fuel to the fire was the water-proofing material used on the tents in those days — a mixture of paraffin and gasoline, both highly combustible. That deadly concoction would nearly sound the death knell for the circus itself less than two years later.

July 4, 1944, the big show was ready to open in Hartford, Conn. North had been replaced as the show's chief executive by Robert Ringling, the son of Edith Ringling and the late Charles, brother of Ringling.

This was all part of the ongoing family struggle for control of the circus that began when John died.

John had changed his will shortly before he died, leaving his house (Ca d'Zan), his art museum and 30 percent interest in the circus to the State of Florida, cutting out the North boys entirely, and leaving just $5,000 to Edith. However, he had not removed the Norths as his executors.

What happened in Hartford that July added to the turmoil. Shortly after 2 p.m, ticket-holders for the afternoon show poured into the giant tent, taking their seats in either the 10 reserved seat areas or the four bleacher sections. Estimates of the crowd that day ranged from 6,000 to 10,000. Circus historian Stewart O'Nan, in his well-researched book, *"The Circus Fire,"* estimated the crowd at 8,700.

The day was hot but that did not deter either the circus fans or the circus performers.

As Merle Evans wielded his baton to strike up the

band, the first production number began, featuring a lion training pretty girls in a role-reversal of what lion-tamers normally did in the center ring. The fearsome lion was really a clown.

Next came the real cat act and then the famous Wallendas, lead by patriarch Karl. They would not finish their act that afternoon, at least not in the normal manner. As they were performing, a tiny fire began in the sidewall of the tent, just behind the southwest bleachers.

Within minutes, the greatest disaster in circus history, happened. For myriad reasons, some of the audience stayed in their seats, unsure what do to, while others, answering to fear, rushed past one or more exits to reach the main entrance where they had entered just minutes earlier.

Evans directed the band to play "Stars and Stripes Forever" as a cue to circus personnel that something was seriously wrong. Their act unfinished, the Wallendas used the rope ladders to escape the high wire. Patrons hastened to leave the tent by a variety of ways, stampeding over those who were less agile as mob mentality took hold, increasing the death count. Waterproofed in the same manner as the menagerie tent in Cleveland in 1942, the big top soon was a sheet of flames, a sheet that too soon settled on a great many people trapped below.

As Emmett Kelly and other performers tried to lead fans to safety, Evans continued to lead the band, until the very last second, before the top came crashing down.

Would this be the final act for the big show? With 167 dead bodies, and charges of criminal negligence filed against five circus employees, this was one of the show's darkest hours.

As the interrogation by officials was stepped up, things grew even bleaker, especially when one of the five men admitted that the show's tent tops had never been fireproofed.

Questions of liability surfaced even before the bodies were buried. The Hartford incident might have even taken a toll in Sarasota. Soon there were more claims against the show than there were assets.

In his book, O'Nan wrote about the show's options. If the circus were forced into receivership, the family would likely lose control of the show and the fire's victims would likely get nothing. If the show declared bankruptcy, it could operate as usual with the likelihood of paying off the victims' claims.

Just one week after the fire, all the circus assets left on the lot in Hartford were seized. While the Ringling managers protested, it became obvious to Ringling family members that something had to be done to save the circus, if only to pay the victims' claims.

To end the deadlock and put the show back on the road, the circus put up nearly $400,000 in cash plus the proceeds of two fire insurance policies. The circus further agreed to use the proceeds from an insurance policy with Lloyd's of London exclusively to pay off claims.

Eight days after the deadly conflagration in Hartford, as workers continued to clean up the site of the great tragedy, the first train, accompanied by a deputy sheriff, headed home to Sarasota. It arrived there four days later, followed by two other sections. The circus had another tent, but, like the tent that had burned, it was waterproof but not fireproof.

With plans for metal seats in a year or so, the Ringling show made plans to go back on the road, without tents, and to play only open-air arenas and ballparks until suitable fireproofing could be had for its tents.

The additional headroom would make for more spectacular circus acts too. Karl Wallenda prepared to take his act to greater heights, perhaps as a precursor of the days when he would walk high above city thoroughfares from one building to another, until eventually he met his death that way in Puerto Rico on March 22,

1978. He had survived the great Hartford fire and even the collapse of the famous seven-man pyramid in Detroit in 1962, but he could not survive a fall from a wire 10 stories over San Juan.

No matter what, the show must go on.

The Wallendas have endured and in 2004, were once again performing their seven-person pyramid.

Like the Wallendas, the Ringling show would endure.

Only the players would change. A new generation of Wallendas walks the wire.

Back in 1944, the Ringling leadership was destined to change again. John Ringling North had been sidelined but he was determined to put himself back in the center ring as man in charge of The Greatest Show on Earth.

With help from Robert Ringling's brother-in-law, James Haley, North managed to get himself back in the driver's seat of the Ringling circus. In 1950, North signed the last of the $4 million in checks paid out after the Hartford fire.

It had been 10 years before the litigation following John Ringling's death was settled and a few more years before the circus recovered from the two fires, but when the dust cleared, Sarasota's future development as the cultural capital of Florida was secure.

The museum and its collection belonged to the state,

deeded by John. That act paved the way for the Asolo Theatre Company, Sarasota Ballet of Florida, the Sarasota Opera and more.

Year in and year out, Sarasota enjoyed its annual Christmas present as the circus returned annually in November, staying through late March until 1959, when the circus announced its intention to move to Venice.

In its Sarasota years, the winter quarters opened its doors to visitors, giving performances each Sunday afternoon and allowing visitors to roam the spacious grounds. People were welcome to visit the menagerie in the big barns, the elephant sheds, the outdoor monkey ranch and other areas.

John and Henry Ringling North, John Ringling's nephews, gave visitors one of the biggest draws of all when they brought Gargantua the Great, an ape that was billed as "the world's most terrifying living creature," to Sarasota.

Rehearsals drew full houses. The layout of the rehearsal area was planned to be just like the layout of Madison Square Garden, where the show opened each year. Surrounded by seats and containing three 42-foot rings and two stages, the area was framed by what everyone called 49th Street along one side and 50th Street along the other. The director would stand on the

49th Street side as the timing of the show was worked out to the split second.

Hundreds of thousands of visitors came to Sarasota each year to see the circus, which soon became the number-one tourist attraction in the state.

During the week, work was the order of the day. Stenos worked at typewriters, bookkeepers bent over their ledgers, schedules were planned, tickets were ordered and posters and programs had to be designed for the new show.

While the show was rehearsing during its winter hiatus in the south, nearly 500 other circus workers were hard at work constructing new costumes, props, animal harnesses and all new tents. Others were repairing wagons, nearly 270 cages, 18 power trucks and 100 railroad cars. Everything was either rebuilt or replaced each year.

Alfred Court, one of the leading trainers during the Sarasota years, rehearsed his jungle-bred animals in the steel arena on the site, while the Cristianis, a family of bareback riders, practiced their acrobatics astride their galloping steeds in another building on the property.

Capt. Hugo Schmitt, working in a shed-like enclosure, made sure his cadre of some 50 elephants toed the mark and responded to his every command.

Broadway choreographer Richard Barstow took all these separate acts and others into consideration as he rehearsed the show's female performers for their roles in the big production numbers that were a trademark of the magnificent extravaganza.

When the show left Sarasota each year to go out on the road, it would visit more than 180 cities. It took eight hours to set up and two hours to tear down, pack

Photo courtesy of Linda Fagan

Broadway choreographer, Richard Barstow, cigarette in hand, leads a rehearsal of one of the productions numbers for which the Ringling Bros. and Barnum & Bailey Circus was famous.

and move on. Such a rigorous schedule would quickly destroy anything made of lower quality materials.

More than 40 people were kept busy feeding the hardworking circus hands. Only the performers paid for their food at winter quarters. All the other circus workers were provided free food and lodging.

In addition to more than 300 performing horses, the circus employed some 400 draft horses. Together, those horses required more than 700 sets of harness. All that was repaired or replaced annually.

Added to the lions, tigers, camels, zebras, hippos and rhinos, the horses became part of what was billed as "the world's largest traveling menagerie."

As long as the circus was performed in tents, as it was during most of the years it wintered in Sarasota, all the tents were replaced annually, a process that consumed miles of canvas, 41 miles of rope and employed nearly 100 people. In addition to stitching the Big Top, which could seat more than 16,000 people, the canvas workers would create animal tents, mess tents and many other circus items made from canvas. Consider that it took 17 acres to hold the layout of tents.

Still other workers were needed to paint the garish sideshow banners, make and sell the pink lemonade and cotton candy and peanuts.

One of the latter employees was Willis Echard Lawson. Born in Connellsville, Pa., Lawson was raised in an orphanage until running away to search for his aunt in Cleveland when he was just 16. Instead, he found the circus and got a job in concessions.

By 1938, he joined the Ringling show, choosing to remain in concessions, becoming assistant manager of the circus in 1947. By 1956 he was the owner of the concessions, a job he held until his retirement in 1972.

Lawson married and raised his two daughters in Sarasota, building his family home on the Hudson Bayou. He was inducted into the Ringling Circus Museum Hall of Fame on Feb. 6, 1998. Also inducted that year were animal trainer Gunther Gebel-Williams and circus trainmaster Charlie Smith.

Lawson died Aug. 1, 2001, just two weeks after the death of Gebel-Williams. Smith and his wife Kitty live in Nokomis. The Smiths were among the honored guests at the rededication of the restored Venice Train Depot on Oct. 24, 2003.

It took four complete trains to move all these people and paraphernalia from town to town. Those train cars were housed on this 200-acre site. They were repaired by Sarasota workers in a large building known as the car shop, also on the circus site.

Circus Days in Sarasota & Venice

The Ringling Bros. and Barnum and Bailey Circus never owned its own locomotives, circus historian and publicist Larry Kellogg said. Train engines are generally owned by the various rail lines and would be changed as the great trains moved from one line's tracks to another line's tracks, Smith said. Instead of engines, elephants often were put into service to move the cars on the siding tracks at winter quarters.

Seaboard Air Line Railway locomotives brought the trains to winter quarters each year and returned to collect the trains when the show was ready to go out on the road again. The same railroad served both Venice

Photo courtesy of Linda Fagan

Willis Lawson, the show's concession chief, animal trainer Gunther Gebel-Williams and trainmaster Charlie Smith were inducted into the Ringling Circus Museum Hall of Fame on Feb. 6, 1998.

and Sarasota. Railroad buffs who want to travel the same rails today may do so at Parrish, Fla. each weekend when members of the Florida Gulf Coast Railroad Museum offer rides in the museum's restored trains.

The track is the same track on which the circus trains traveled to Sarasota and, from 1960 to 1992, to Venice.

Tickets can be purchased at the rail station in Parrish.

Each Ringling circus train car was at least 70 feet in length. They ranged from flatbed cars to stock cars, elephant cars and sleeper cars. The performers' cars were fitted according to one's status in the show, with the stars being housed in splendor, generally in their own car or major portion of a car.

Lesser circus performers would be allotted portions of rail cars or maybe even just sleeping space in a shared compartment. While accommodations might vary in size, every space was created from the finest materials. So was every tent, every animal blanket and every costume.

There was a dormitory for performers, a complete blacksmith shop, wardrobe- and harness-making buildings, pools for some of the animals, a hospital, dining hall, stables, indoor and outdoor cages, a giraffe house, canvas storage building, offices and more.

There was little if any wasted space at Ringling's 200-acre winter quarters site in Sarasota.

Circus entertains during WWII

As important as the circus was to Sarasota, it may have been even more so to the United States during World War II.

One of the most unique bits of memorabilia in the collection of Sarasota circus fan Bob Horne is a framed copy of a letter that John and Henry Ringling North issued to all the associates of the circus.

In the letter, the brothers explained the special treatment being accorded to the circus in return for what the circus was doing for the morale of the country during those trying times.

The text of the letter is as follows:

The management of the Ringling Brothers and Barnum & Bailey Circus thinks it timely and fitting to state its policy and hopes for the future in this critical period in our national history. Through letters from many individuals, wide editorial comment from the nation's press and direct expressions from the country's Army, Navy and political leaders, it has been that the public wants The Greatest Show on Earth to carry on during war time. Everyone cannot shoulder a gun, nor is everyone expected to. Many millions must work at home, in factory, field and office to supply and maintain our armies and our boats. These millions must have diversion when released from their labors and so far it has been our duty and privilege to help in providing such diversions.

Our local draft board in Sarasota, and other boards throughout the country, including the central office of the Selective Service System in Washington, have been more sympathetic and cooperative in granting deferments for key workers and performers.

The War Production Board too, is doing its part in making our continued operations possible through granting us priority for materials essential to maintenance and supply.

President Roosevelt has personally expressed his appreciation of the fact that the Show is Going On.

Several letters arrive each week from former employees now in the various armed services wanting to know how business is, wanting to be remembered to former bosses and friends, hoping that we will keep the cookhouse flag flying and that they CAN BE WITH IT again when we have won and when the war is over.

Hard and trying days are ahead for all of us, but such prospects have never before chilled American spirits or stopped American Initiative and we feel that as long as those two qualities are alive, the American Circus, too, will roll on ... on to provide entertainment for the public, employment for our own kind, and an example of cooperation, skill and imagination which is unique in the field of entertainment, and of which all of us who are part of it may well be proud.

And so our policy — Advance planning and preparation to make next year's show Bigger and Better than Ever in Quality and Spirit, if not in size. And to hope that Our circus will continue just as our American Way of Life certainly will!

John and Henry Ringling North

When the war was over, America got back to business. Rosie the Riveter went back to her children and the circus could once again concentrate on becoming bigger in size as well as in spirit.

It was only a matter of time until the bigger and better circus would be noticed by Hollywood and its Sarasota winter quarters and even the city itself would be immortalized on the Silver Screen.

Hollywood stars arrive

Cecil B. DeMille's 1952 Oscar Award-winning film, "The Greatest Show on Earth," was filmed on location in Sarasota, bringing still more acclaim to the city. Most

of the outdoor scenes were
filmed at the winter quarters,
bringing many of the film's
stars to the city by the bay for
weeks at a time.

"Jimmy Stewart was the
one major star who never
came to Sarasota for the film-
ing," circus historian Bob
Horne said. "The train wreck
was shot with a miniature
train belonging to Howard
Tibbals, the man who recently
donated his miniature circus layout to the Circus Museum."

Photo by Kim Cool

**Howard Tibbals in a
hard hat on the con-
struction site of the
Tibbals Learning Center
at the Ringling museum
complex in Sarasota.**

(The 3,660-square foot miniature circus will be dis-
played in the 30,600-square foot Tibbals Learning Center
addition to the Circus Museum. Considered the world's
most spectacular model of the American circus, the layout will be used to provide interactive learning oppor-
tunities for children of all ages. It also will augment university programs. The completion of the Tibbals
Learning Center, scheduled to open in Sept. 2005, effec-
tively doubles the size of the Ringling Museum of the
Circus.)

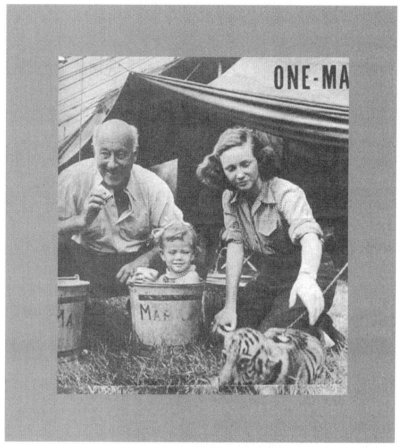

Photo courtesy of Linda Fagan

When this photo of Sarasota native Linda Lawson Fagan
was taken in 1951, she was small enough to fit in an animal feeding bucket at the Sarasota winter quarters of the
Ringling Bros. Barnum & Bailey Circus. At left is the
Academy Award-winning film director Cecil B. DeMille
who was in Sarasota to film "The Greatest Show on
Earth," which was named Best Picture in 1952 and
earned an Oscar nomination for DeMille as Best Director.
At right, petting one of the circus's baby tigers, is an
unknown assistant of DeMille's.

43

More than 350,000 visitors tour the Museum of the Circus annually — another winter quarters legacy.

Full-sized circus train cars that had been in a real train wreck in California were repainted to look like Ringling cars for the train wreck aftermath, Horne said. They provided the backdrop for the scene in which Jimmy Stewart's character, Buttons the Clown, is recognized as a wanted killer by a detective when Buttons stays to save the life of Brad, the circus owner, who was injured in the wreck.

Brad was played by Charlton Heston.

Besides the train wreck, the film had a cast of thousands, a love triangle, great spectacle, drama and melodrama, uncredited cameos of Bob Hope and Bing Crosby and 182 minutes of glorious Technicolor. Mickey Mouse and Donald Duck appeared in a production number, a forerunner of future joint ventures between Feld Entertainment and the Walt Disney Company.

Among the circus acts in the film's circus were famous clown Lou Jacobs, Felix Adler, Paul Jung, the Flying Concellos, the Maxellos and Dolores Hall.

Art Concello, a former trapeze flyer with great business accumen that would prove useful to the famous circus less than a decade later, designed Cornel Wilde's (The Great Sebastian) famous fall and tested it.

"He was a great flyer," Horne said about Concello. "He

figured out how to do the fall so that no one would get hurt. He got paid for the stunt and for doing it."

Horne said the film crew dug a deep hole, coverd it with a trapeze net, which they camouflaged with leaves and dirt. Overnight, it rained. The hole, unbeknownst to anyone, filled with water. Concello did the fall the next day.

"He came up out of the hoke spitting mud and stuff and said, 'shoot it.',", Horne said.

In the film, Fae Alexander did the fall.

"He had broken his neck before but no one saw the break on the X-ray until three months later," Horne said. "So he actually did the fall with a broken neck."

While Alexander was swinging through the air with the greatest of ease, Wilde was doing his trapeze swinging bits just six inches above a stage, with the camera shooting from below. Clown Jackie LeClaire, a former aerialist, doubled for Wilde on all his other trapeze tricks, Horne said.

Paramount Studios paid the Ringling show $250,000 in 1949 for the rights to the circus' name, use of its equipment and the stars named above. The payoff for this investment was worldwide fame for Sarasota and accolades and Oscars for DeMille, the film's director.

In 1952, "The Greatest Show on Earth" earned DeMille an Academy Award nomination as Best Director and two Academy Awards: Best Picture and

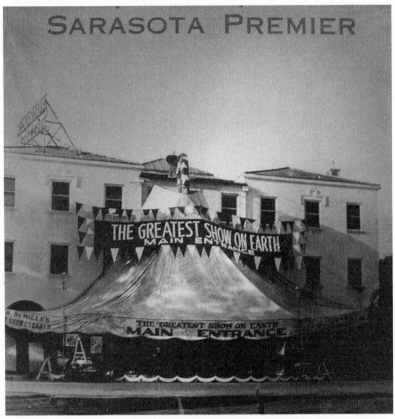

From a display of the Ringling Museum of the Circus

For the world premier of the Cecil B. DeMille film, "The Greatest Show on Earth," the former Edwards Theatre entrance was draped in a large circus tent. Most of the stars came to the premier of the Academy Award-winning film, which made Sarasota internationally famous overnight.

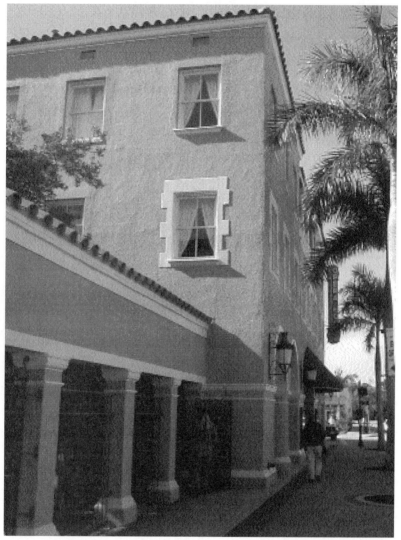

Photo by Kim Cool

The Sarasota Opera House, originally built in 1926 as the Edwards Theater, at 61 N. Pineapple Ave., was the site of the world premier of the 1952 Academy Award-winning film, "The Greatest Show on Earth." It now is home to the Sarasota Opera Company.

47

Best Motion Picture Story. To win the Oscar, the film had to beat out four motion picture classics: "High Noon," "Ivanhoe," "Moulin Rouge" and "The Quiet Man."

One of its stars, Gloria Graham, did win an Oscar that year for Best Supporting Actress, but for another film, "The Bad and the Beautiful."

Many of the stars, including Cornel Wilde, Betty Hutton, Charlton Heston and Dorothy Lamour, returned for the film's world premier at the former Edwards Theater.

The theater's name had been changed to the Florida Theater prior to 1952 and then was renamed again for its present use as the home of the Sarasota Opera. For the premier, world-famous clown Emmett Kelly led the circus parade to the theater. Once again, thanks to the most famous circus of all, Sarasota's economy profited and, most of all, its fame was spread far and wide.

The next year was the 27th season in Sarasota. Millions of visitors had seen rehearsals and preview shows there. With the success of the film, still more circus fans would find their way to Sarasota, especially during the three months when the show was at its winter quarters.

In those years, the circus would arrive at winter quarters late in November, staying until March, when it

would head to New York to debut the new show at
Madison Square Garden.

Each Sunday throughout those winter months,
beginning the first Sunday in December, the circus
would stage special matinee performances for visitors.

These visitors would be the first to see the new acts
hired for the coming season. They also would be first to
see the reworked or new acts by returning performers.
While on the property, visitors were allowed to roam
the grounds, visit the menagerie in the barns, visit the
elephant sheds, horse barns, monkey ranch and watch
the various trainers in action. Shows were given only on
Sundays but the grounds were open to visitors seven
days a week.

Daily, visitors witnessed the work that went into
making the show a marvel of split-second timing. Acts
rehearsed over and over again. Painters decorated the
wagons. Flat cars were repaired; costumes were sewn;
tents were stitched; cats went through their routines;
and many of the menagerie animals appeared bored
while clowns did their routines without makeup.

John Ringling North, nephew of the man who
brought the show to Sarasota, spent his days nearby in
the private railroad car named for his Uncle John and
Aunt Mable.

Artists swelled the ranks of the visitors to the winter quarters. The artists came in search of the color and the myriad subjects to be found there. Their creations were showcased in a special Circus Show sponsored by the Sarasota Art Association and held annually at the John and Mable Ringling Museum of Art.

The city by the bay owed much to the Ringling Bros. and Barnum & Bailey Circus. It was a match made in heaven and one that seemed likely to last forever.

An era ends

The match made in heaven would last just four more years. On July 16, 1956, in Pittsburgh, the Big Top was taken down for the last time.

Television had caught on in a big way. People could stay home and see circus acts up close on their 12-inch black and white sets. The novelty of the flickering image more than compensated for the lack of color.

Ed Sullivan and other TV stars of that era were bringing entertainment into the home, and the homes were being built out where the circus once set up its tents, outside of town. There was a name for the new areas being developed — "suburbia." With fewer places to pitch its tents and fewer customers, the giant tent show had to fall back and regroup or die.

Cutting its losses and limping home earlier than usual that year, the circus did not sit back and lick its wounds in the tropical sunshine. Nor did Sarasota, which shared the economic pains being experienced by the circus. Many Sarasota jobs were lost. When the circus moved indoors, performing in large arenas rather than in tents, there was no more need for tentmakers. Fewer train cars were needed, fewer animals were needed, fewer performers were needed and soon there would be little need for the 200-acre site in Sarasota.

It was a leaner and meaner circus that went on the road the next year — mostly in trucks. It seemed as though the tent era and the train era were ending at the same time.

As trucking lines prospered, delivering goods to the new suburbs, railroads and tracks began to disappear and, in many places, including Sarasota, even the depots would be torn down.

Stadiums and arenas were the new venues. Trucks seemed the logical means to move the show from town to town.

"We're building an indoor ballpark show," Concello said to Charlie Smith, a man who had built several circuses since first working for Ben Davenport as a performer and jack-of-all-trades in the Princess Iola Vanity

Photo by Kim Cool

On Jan. 18, 2004, Art Concello was inducted into the
Sarasota Circus Ring of Fame for his many contributions
to circus. During the ceremony, Concello was credited with
keeping the show (Ringling Bros. and Barnum & Bailey
Circus) open during its lean times in 1956-57 and then
guiding the show's rebirth as it became an arena show.
Shown are his widow, Margaret Concello, daughter-in-law
Carol, granddaughter Antoinette and great-grandson,
Shawn, 5, moments before the plaque unveiling in Sarasota.

Photo courtesy of Charlie Smith

Ringling trainmaster Charlie Smith takes a rare respite from his duties as the trainmaster of the Red Unit of The Greatest Show on Earth in 1977, the year he was honored by Illinois-based circus fans who chartered the Charlie Smith tent for the CFA.

53

Kim Cool

Fair Co., Davenport Society Circus and Daily Bros. Circus.

Smith's circus career began in 1934 and continued until his retirement from The Greatest Show on Earth in 1995. Except for a few years in the U.S. Navy and a few other years off, he spent his life in the circus.

He was ready for another break from circus life

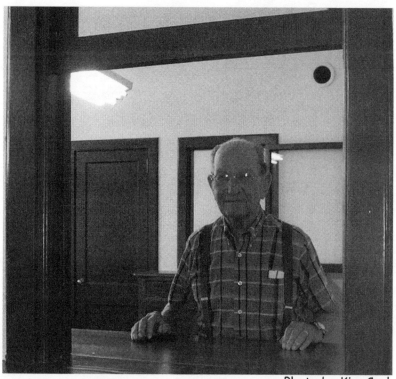

Photo by Kim Cool

On Oct. 24, 2003, former Ringling trainmaster Charlie Smith checked out the ticket booth of the rededicated and recently restored Venice Train Depot, the depot where he brought The Greatest Show on Earth for most of its Venice years.

when Concello persuaded him to do "some welding."
"That's how I joined the Ringling show," he said.

It was somewhat ironic that the man who would be trainmaster for the Ringling show longer than anyone else actually spent his early Ringling years converting the show to a truck show, using the experience he had from the 72-truck King Bros. Circus.

Nearly 50 years later, Concello and Smith were inducted into the Sarasota Circus Ring of Fame on the same day, Jan. 19, 2004. Smith received a standing ovation from those present.

"Charlie represented the many variations of the American Shows, from wagons to railroads," longtime performer John Herriott said while speaking about Smith. "Charlie has done it all."

Circus education research project director, clown and performance director, Peggy Williams, said that Smith had become a legend in both the circus and the railroad industries.

Concello's family accepted the award on behalf of the man who also had become a legend.

Financially strapped and eschewing tents entirely for the new indoor venues, the circus turned over its booking chores to independent agents and promoters. One of these, by the name of Irvin Feld, was one of the leading

Charlie and Kitty Smith, above, at their home in Nokomis, Fla., display a model of the circus train car on which they lived for 16 years while he was the trainmaster for the Ringling Bros. and Barnum & Bailey Circus. In photo below, Kitty Smith points to the model of the compartment in which they lived. It had a washer and dryer.

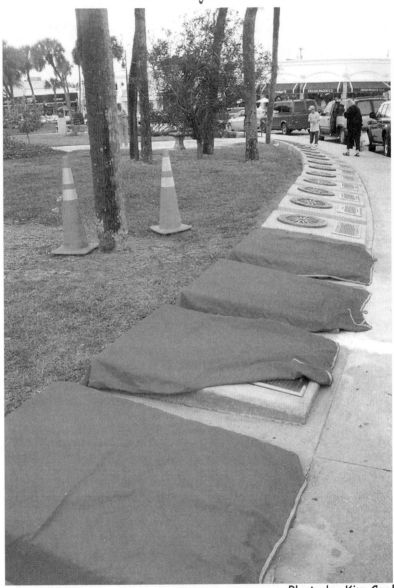

Photo by Kim Cool

Four plaques were unveiled at the Sarasota Circus Ring of Fame in 2004 to honor (from the bottom) Charlie Smith, Galla Shawn, Art Concello and the Konyot family.

rock 'n roll promoters in the country. He knew the inside and outside of these new venues better than anyone.

Change became the mantra of the Ringling show. Gone were the tents, most of the train cars, traveling hotels and restaurants, resident booking agents and ticket sellers. Even the schedule was drastically changed.

Only the month-long engagement at Madison Square Garden remained untouched. One-night stands were dropped in favor of longer engagements in the bigger cities. The change was done partly by necessity because few if any of the smaller towns had indoor venues of a size to accommodate even the stripped-down show and partly because of the expense and work of setting up and tearing down the arena-style show.

The show would come into a place like Cleveland's Arena and perform to full houses for at least a week. It drew its audience from the whole northeastern part of Ohio. When the show played Columbus, it again would draw from a larger area, bypassing the small towns it once had visited in the central part of the state.

For the first three and one-half years that the new scaled-down show was on the road, it literally was "on the road," moving primarily by truck, with only a small menagerie and a few performers and other personnel traveling in a few leased train cars. Both rail stock and the 12 trucks sported the Ringling logo on their sides.

Outdoor rigging was carried in trucks for use in towns without indoor arenas. In those places, the circus would set up its equipment before fairground grandstands or ball parks.

Smith traveled with the train during these important years when the show was being rebuilt. He was the per-

Photo by Kim Cool

From left, Kitty Smith; retired Ringling trainmaster Charlie Smith; Carol (Mrs. Randall Concello), Art Concello's second wife, Margaret; and his son, Randall Concello, with the awards presented to Smith and the Concello family by the Sarasota Circus Ring of Fame in 2004 on St. Armands Circle in Sarasota.

fect man for the job. In 1946 he built the Rogers Bros. Circus. From 1949 to 1950, he worked as the lot superintendent and boss canvasman for the Mickey Dale Circus, before moving on to set up the big top and operate the pie car for the Little Bob Stevens Circus.

Finally, in 1954, he got the job that gave him the best preparation for what loomed ahead when he joined Ringling — he was the transportation superintendent on Floyd King's 72-truck King Bros. Circus. Smith left the cash-poor King Circus in 1955, joining the Clyde Beatty-Cole Bros. Circus in 1956, the last year it would travel by rail. With three months' rail experience, his truck experiences and decades in the circus, Smith was the perfect man to help rebuild the Ringling show. Smith lived aboard the train, overseeing the loading and unloading of passengers and wagons, but he also supervised the truck fleet. (*There will be more about Smith in the following chapter*)

Rockin' and Rollin' along

With Smith moving the circus along on rail and road and independent contractor Feld contributing advice about the new venues, things were looking up. At this point a jolt of new money was just what the show needed to finish its transformation.

The answer was in Sarasota. The circus had put the

town on the map, enriching the city and now the city would enrich the circus. Developers were clamoring for land as the next Florida land boom was about to get under way. Ringling's winter quarters property was the answer to its money woes.

Sarasota's first mayor, A.B. Edwards had paid $4 per acre for the property in 1912. It was used for celery farming in those days before becoming the site of the county fairgrounds. Fair buildings had been converted

Photo courtesy of Linda Lawson Fagan

For more than 30 years, The Greatest Show on Earth wintered on the site of the former Sarasota County Fairgrounds, off Beneva Road and across the street from the Bobby Jones Golf Course. The 200-acre site is now covered with homes built since 1963.

to house circus animals but finally the time had come to house people on what had become a prime piece of Sarasota real estate.

Reduced to just 40 units, and redesigned for indoor spaces, the circus could use the money from the sale of its 200 acres of valuable property far better than it could use the land itself.

There was some brief discussion by the Board of the County Commissioners in 1959 as to the ownership of the land, but that ended when the county historian, Doris Davis, found an entry that indicated "beyond question that the Board of County Commissioners in 1925, when they went into possession of these lands, did so as a lessee under the County Agricultural Fair Association whose leasehold was transferred to the circus when it acquired the property."

When county attorney Donald C. McCleland Jr. presented a piece of paper describing the land and stating: "This land shall belong to John Ringling, or his heirs, forever," the matter was settled.

The land was sold by the circus to Arvida Realty Co. for what was believed to be $350,000. Later the property was sold to Paver Development Company.

With money in the bank and John Ringling North still figuratively at the helm, the Ringling show interrupted its 1960 season to return to an all-rail format and make its last stop in Sarasota.

Headliners continued to drive from city to city in their own house trailers but the rest of the show would travel in style aboard a new 15-car train, which was emblazoned on all sides with the Ringling logo. In August the train left Sarasota for the last time as it headed out to complete its 1960 tour.

Lloyd Morgan, an old-timer with Ringling and already a legend, was the trainmaster, but Smith was at his side, adding to the knowledge he had gained from the King Bros. and Clyde Beatty shows.

When it headed south for the coming winter, it would travel to Venice.

All that remains of the winter quarters of the Ringling circus' 1927-1959 residency in Sarasota is a sign near the corner of Beneva Road and Calliandra Drive.

The marker was erected in 1983. That was more than 20 years after the circus vacated the site and moved to Venice. The sign was donated by the Sarasota County Historical Society. It was dedicated by animal trainer and former performance director John Herriott, who was president of Show Folks of America that year.

Years later, in 2004, serving as master of ceremonies for Circus Celebrity Night at the Ringling Museum of the Circus, Herriott said, "As a relocated circus person, when we get up every morning in January and

February, we say 'Thank you, John Ringling. If not for you we would be in Baraboo or Bridgeport, freezing our ... off.'"

"There'll never be anything like it in this world," former circus veterinarian, "Doc" J.Y. Henderson, said at the dedication.

He was not alone in saying that the Sarasota winter quarters were the largest, most elaborate and best-known circus facilities in the world.

The site also was the most visited, something that most likely will never happen again. More recently, Jenny Wallenda echoed those sentiments, saying there would never be such a wonderful place for the circus performers.

"I know the circus seems vast, with so many segments," Willis Lawson's daughter, Linda Fagan, said. "I like to think of the big top days at Ringling as the golden era, a special time. Circus people were like family to each other, all different nationalities, right after the war when people banned together. Hollywood seemed a bit more special and less showy in those days, not like now when everyone seems to be a star and do anything to keep their name in the limelight. A lot of the real stars avoid the press and the limelight."

Fagan has a special collection of memorabilia that includes photos of the Concellos, film stars Burt Lancaster and David Jansen (as a horsewalker with her mother on the horse).

"I heard that DeMille once asked my father to come to Hollywood to work behind the scenes (my dad was not an in-front-of-the-scenes type person) so if he went I could have been a Hollywood brat instead of a circus brat!"

The 200-acre parcel that once housed tents and trains, performers, concessionaires and costume makers connected with The Greatest Show on Earth, is today the site of Glen Oaks Estates, which opened in 1963 as one of the featured locations of that year's Parade of Homes.

Although the remains of buried circus animals are said to still be on the property, the only visible marker that The Greatest Show on Earth once was there is that marker at the Beneva Road entrance to Glen Oaks. It can be found in the median of Calliandra Drive, just inside the entrance to the subdivision.

As the circus was smaller when it left Sarasota, so was the historical society marker smaller than the giant signs that once proclaimed to one and all that the site was the winter home of The Greatest Show on Earth.

Also smaller was the new winter quarters in Venice.

When the circus arrived at its new winter quarters on Dec. 27, 1960, after completing the 1960 tour, it arrived by truck caravan at a 15-acre site, not a 200-acre spread.

Kim Cool

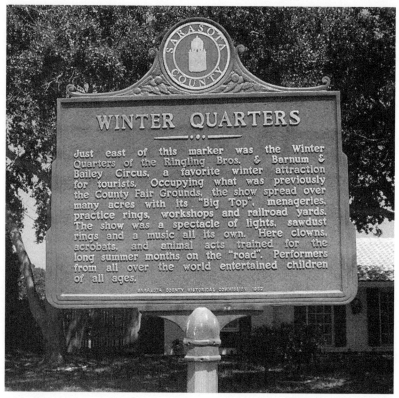

Photo by Kim Cool

At the Beneva Road entrance to Glen Oaks is the only
reminder that The Greatest Show on Earth once wintered
in Sarasota. Beneath the words "WINTER QUARTERS,"
is the following inscription: "Just east of this marker was
the Winter Quarters of the Ringling Bros. & Barnum &
Bailey Circus, a favorite winter attraction for tourists.
Occupying what was previously the County Fair Grounds,
the show spread over many acres with its "Big Top,"
menageries, practice rings, workshops and railroad yards.
The Show was a spectacle of lights, sawdust rings and a
music all its own. Here, clowns, acrobats and animal acts
trained for the long summer months on the "road."
Performers from all over the world entertained children
of all ages."

The new space was smaller than just the area used in Sarasota to set up the tents when the circus was still a tent show.

Newspapers of the day referred to the show as a Christmas gift for Venice.

The *Venice Gondolier Sun* proclaimed in an editorial, "Yes Venice, there is a Santa Claus."

In the copy, the writer pointed out the fact that the name of Venice would be on every circus release sent to newspapers all over the country, something that would be good for the tourist business.

Most of the movers and shakers in Sarasota were sad to see the circus go but could not come up with the land needed by the show, even though it needed far less than the 200 acres it had occupied for the previous 32 years.

Sarasota Mayor Frank L. Hoersting said the circus had been a big asset to the city but that he doubted its departure would hurt the city "one bit."

"Since they folded up their big tent show, sold their animals and quit having their big Sunday shows, it has not been as great a tourist attraction as before," he said.

Was this downsizing an omen, or would it prove to be a blessing? Fewer jobs would be created by this smaller show. As some people in Venice felt that some people associated with the circus were undesirable transients, smaller was better in their opinion.

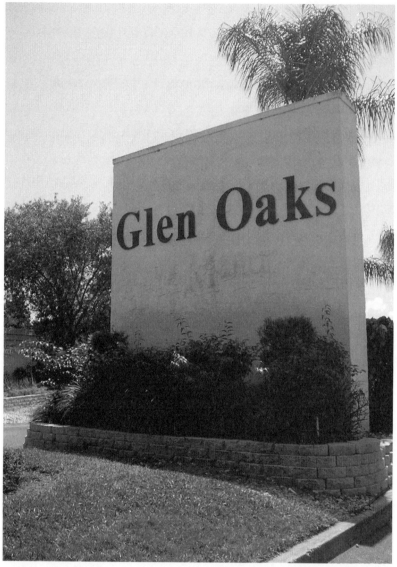

Photo by Kim Cool

The entrance to Glen Oaks, an Arvida development of
middle class homes that was built on the site of the former
winter quarters of the Ringling Bros. and Barnum &
Bailey Circus in Sarasota.

A Mrs. Gonzalez who was the owner of the Circus City Trailer Park in Sarasota, was quoted in one newspaper article of the day saying that circus people like to live among their own and that those people who regularly travel thousands of miles per year would not hesitate to drive just 20 miles to the new location. She said that many circus people traveled in their own trailers when the show was on tour.

Most of the performers were described as family oriented home-owners who placed their children in county schools and valued education.

Superintendent of Public Instruction Carl Strode said that circus performers are very fine people and "the children of circus families are very good students."

One Sarasota business owner was sad to see the show leave town. He was the owner of the Sinclair service station on the road to the circus quarters.

"I hate to see the circus leave, it brings a lot of people out here," said the man identified only as Bowers in a paper of the day. "Even though it has not been open to the public for some time, many people drive out here past the grounds just to say they saw the circus headquarters.

"In the old days when they had the animals and everything, hundreds came out every day, so you know

I will miss the business. Don't let anyone tell you the circus hurt anyone, it helped Sarasota a lot."

Whether there would be new jobs or not, the notoriety alone might be enough to make the move worthwhile to the city of Venice, where there was one other major contrast between its circus site and the old 200-acre Sarasota site.

The Venice location was much more public, backing up as it did to the Tamiami Trail, along the eastern edge of the city's 1,100-acre airport property.

Anyone heading south out of the city would pass the arena.

That remained true even after the opening of the Intracoastal Waterway that made an island of most of Venice in 1967.

The airport and the circus arena were on the island, nearly adjacent to the south bridge over the waterway.

The site would prove handy in 2003-4 as a work-staging area when the roadway was widened and two new bridges were built to replace the old span. There would even be an entrance to the former circus property from the widened road.

As this book went to press, plans were being made for an office park to be built on the former circus grounds.

Following the Sarasota land sale and the move to the

new site, the Ringling Bros. and Barnum & Bailey Circus was about ready to be reborn yet again.

"It made Sarasota and it can do the same of Venice," said Todd Swaim, manager of the Sarasota Chamber of Commerce and its executive secretary. "It's like history repeating itself. If we had to lose the circus, I'm glad it stayed in the county."

Follow the money

That the circus had survived at all may have been the miracle of 1956.

Arriving back in Sarasota on July 18, 1956, after a shortened season, the circus languished for several months. The animals were cared for but nearly every human was dismissed. Things were in such disarray that Charles and Edith Ringling's descendants filed a lawsuit against the two North brothers and Art

Concello, claiming mismanagement and breach of fiduciary duty.

Like the earlier lawsuits that had tied up the John Ringling estate for some 10 years after the great showman's death in 1936, the 1956 Ringling lawsuit would drag on nearly as long.

While that scenario played itself out in court, it was Concello who would guide the show through those trying times in the late 1950s.

It would have been tough enough to condense a three-ring extravaganza to fit an indoor arena but it would be years before every town would have an arena. Until then, the giant circus would have to be flexible enough to play arenas where they existed and even ball parks in some locales. The performance tent was gone. Ingenuity was needed.

John Ringling North needed Concello. He needed him enough that he basically gave Concello carte blanche to do whatever he wanted to with the circus.

Circus historian Fred D. Pfening Jr. was quoted as saying the show became "Concello Bros. all the way."

When the show went on the road for the 1957 season, it was a smaller troupe. When the big performance tent came down for the last time, the need for so many train cars ended as well. Just 15 train cars would be used.

The train took a smaller menagerie and equipment to New York, and then on to Boston. Trucks hauled everything else. An old school bus that once transported personnel from the train to the show lot was used as a circus office, its final incarnation.

It was the beginning of the final decade of Ringling ownership and management.

It also was the beginning of the downsizing of the winter quarters.

Winter quarters had spread out over some 200 acres during the Ringling show's Sarasota years, becoming home to the performers in the off season. Even today, more than 40 years after the great show pulled out of the city, Sarasota retains strong ties to the circus via the performers and other circus employees who continue to call Sarasota home.

No longer requiring room for tentmakers or the room to pitch the huge tents and house herds of wild animals, the circus could get along with much less — 185 acres less as it turned out.

The circus collected more than $350,000 for the sale of the Sarasota property. It would be paying the city of Venice just $1,000 per year in rent and could use that $350,000 to build what it needed in Venice.

The new home would cover just 15 acres along U.S.

41 on airport property in Venice, although it did have an option on an additional 80 acres. The additional acreage would be necessary only if the circus decided to go ahead with plans to build a $1 million circus-inspired theme park. The initial lease was to run for 30 years with an option for a 20-year extension.

"It's bigger than anything Venice has ever had,"

Photo courtesy of the Venice Archives and Area Historical Collection
The Venice Circus Arena parking lot would fill each time the Ringling Bros. and Barnum & Bailey Circus would hold its preview shows before going out on the road for the new season. Photo taken in the early 1970s.

75

Venice Area Chamber of Commerce president H. N. "Bud" Wimmers said about the deal that would bring the winter quarters of The Greatest Show on Earth to Venice. Wimmers had successfully brought the Kentucky Military Institute winter quarters to Venice in 1932. He had been a major player in the development of South Venice in the 1950s. He landed the biggest fish of all when he set up negotiations between the circus and the city just minutes after the circus had failed to meet the deadline in its negotiations for a new home in Sarasota.

That deadline had passed on a Thursday and by Friday at 11:30 p.m., the Venice deal had been struck, including the approval of the city council. The following Wednesday at noon, Mayor Smythe Brohard and City Clerk Lewis A. Hester signed the 30-year lease, which had been prepared by City Attorney M. A. Braswell. Then the lease was mailed off to the circus's New York City office for additional signatures, with a copy to the Federal Aviation Authority. The FAA had to approve the deal because it involved airport property but FAA approval was considered a "mere formality" according to newspaper reports of the time.

From the minute the document was signed, there were Venice residents who were sure the circus got the better part of the deal, but both sides had bargained well and the circus was required to do far more than simply pay rent.

In return for its modest rent, the circus was required to have no other winter quarters save Venice, and, whenever practical, "designate Venice, Fla. as the head-quarters and winter home of Ringling, at least to the same extent as Sarasota has been heretofore so designated." The circus also was expected to begin construction of "one or more structures and other improvements for storage, rehearsal and other circus and exhibition purposes, including wardrobe — costume shop and general offices, storage building and rehearsal arena of sufficient size to rehearse the circus with capacity for seating approximately 5,000 spectators." Some 30 years later when the circus was again considering a change of venue for its winter quarters, one of the reasons cited was the city's requirement to reduce the number of seats by 1,000 because of fire codes.

Even though the circus was smaller and needed far less acreage, it still was dependent on the rail lines to move from place to place.

It would never have come to Venice had the rail line not been there and it would not stay in the city if there ever came a time when the rail line no longer serviced

Venice, an unlikely scenario considering that the city had been developed by the Brotherhood of Locomotive Engineers back in the mid 1920s. (Hold that thought.)

At the Sarasota site, there had been room for four 25-car trains on six sidings as well as a rail car repair building and two separate rail lines into and out of the winter quarters property.

In Venice, in 1960, all the circus required was a rail-road spur and space to park 25 rail cars on the premises — gleaming new train cars. Already marked with their Venice, Florida labels, the new train cars were seen for the last time at the Sarasota Luke Wood Park siding of the Seaboard line between Washington Boulevard and Osprey Avenue. It was the end of July 1960, prior to the train's departure for Omaha, Neb., where the show would perform Aug. 4 and 5 that year.

In addition to the new location name on the side of the train, the train cars themselves were different.

According to an article in the *Sarasota Herald Tribune* of July 31, that year, seven of the 15 train cars would be tunnel cars that could each hold as many as five circus wagons. Wagons are pulled into the tunnel cars by trac-tors like those used at airports to pull planes into place. The new system was developed by Art Concello, the general manager of the big show, and trainmaster Lloyd

Morgan.

The circus got the Venice railroad spur and sidings as part of the deal.

What it did not get was all the living space it had had for performers, families and animals in Sarasota.

The new winter quarters would be home to the circus and its train cars but would not necessarily be home to its workers, whether performers or otherwise. House trailers were forbidden under the terms of the contract except for animal trainers during rehearsal season. Animals also were not welcome, except during rehearsal season.

Brohard noted that "the circus will be Venice's first major tourist attraction and ... the circus is following the trend of the population to the southern end of the county."

That trend continues to this day.

Brohard also expressed the hope that the circus would recognize that growth trend and respond in a positive manner by building its proposed year-round tourist attraction.

The tourist attraction would never be built if the circus could not come to Venice. In a March 23, 1960 article in the *Sarasota News*, it was reported that "a possible roadblock has been raised by the Federal Aviation

Administration over a plan by the Ringling Bros. and Barnum & Bailey Circus to relocate its winter quarters in Venice."

Brohard was quoted in the article, confirming that people opposed to the circus having its winter quarters in Venice have stirred up a controversy over the proposed lease of airport land.

"Main point is the fact that the FAA has raised a question as to whether the $1,000-a-year rent for 15 acres is sufficient."

An even bigger objection was voiced against giving the circus first refusal on an option to lease an additional 80 acres on the east side of the airport and south of the 15-acre main parcel. When the option clause was dropped, a 30-year contract for the circus site was signed, including a clause calling for review of the contract every five years, and the $1,000 rental adjusted according to the federal government's "cost-of-living" standard. The revised contract was signed April 29, 1960.

Construction of the 5,000-seat arena began immediately and enough of the building was finished in time to hold the 1961 rehearsals there. The four-story, 55,000-square-foot building was totally finished before the fall of 1962. It was the third largest arena in Florida at that time. The population of the city of Venice was 5,100.

Cost of the completed arena was predicted to be $100,000 but, by the time of its completion, was estimated to be nearly three times that amount. Several additional buildings were built, resulting in the circus spending more in Venice than it had received for its Sarasota property. While the city would be receiving just $1,000 in annual rent, it would be the recipient of all these buildings should the circus ever vacate the airport site and it also would benefit from the publicity generated by the circus being housed there.

With predictions of increased tourist spending and new jobs in the city, the economic implications of the arrival of the circus seemed positive.

But if the circus failed, all bets were off and the city might be left with a new but empty arena.

Would history repeat itself?

Venice had already seen one other circus come and go since the end of World War II.

In 1946, Venice Mayor Clyde V. Higel had signed a lease with the Sparks Circus, which was planning to establish its winter quarters in Venice. That circus leased a large hangar and two T-shaped barracks left over from the days when the airport was an army air base. The circus augmented the buildings with tents that were set up on the same land where the Ringling circus would erect its arena 14 years later.

In February 1947, the new green Sparks performance tent was raised along the Tamiami Trail and invitations went out for residents and others to come to a dress rehearsal, with proceeds of the March 2, 1947 show earmarked for the No-Vel Post No. 159 of the American Legion. The brand-new tent was no match for the rains that deluged Venice that day and continued to dog the Sparks Circus for much of its run that season. By the time the show limped into Tacoma, Washington, in September, it had lost performers who had deserted what seemed a sinking ship along the route. It gave its last performance in Tacoma Sept. 7 that year.

Although the Sparks Circus never returned to Venice, its owner, James Edgar, had put Venice on the circus map.

While the much larger Ringling show was less likely to be swamped by bad weather, it was a circus in the throes of reorganization when it arrived at its new Venice home in late fall of 1960.

Nearly completed that fall was a new 55,000-square-foot arena. Nearly four stories in height, the building was destined to become a landmark in Venice for sever-

Photo courtesy of the Venice Archives and Area Historical Collection

No sooner was the ink dry on its contract with the city of Venice than the Ringling Bros. and Barnum & Bailey Circus began to build a new circus arena that would be used as a rehearsal hall for training purposes and as a venue in which to stage its annual preview productions before going on the road with the new show each spring. When completed, the building held 5,000 seats, room for three show rings and offices for circus executives.

al decades to come. Like the new-styled train cars, the arena had been designed by Concello and Morgan. The arena would have two 60-foot wings and adjacent buildings housing staging, costumes and wardrobe space.

Seating that could be lifted up and out of the way to maximize the floor space for trade shows or ventures other than the circus and its rehearsals was designed by Charlie Smith who, like many of the great circus employees, was somewhat of a jack-of-all-trades. Smith had begun his seven-decade circus career in 1934 in a combination medicine show/circus.

"We did vaudeville acts in the winter and circus acts in the summer," he said.

For 10 years, he danced in drag, did a knife-throwing act (aiming at his first wife), helped with the canvas, and served as a mechanic and sideshow concessionaire.

Drafted, he served in the United States Navy during World War II. Smith returned to circus life in 1946, building the Rogers Bros. Circus and the Stevens Bros. Circus for two seasons before spending two years in his wife's hometown, Gonzales, Texas, where he ran a saloon for two years. He then returned to the road with the King Bros. Circus and the Clyde Beatty Circus before joining the Ringling Show.

His varied experiences proved helpful as he designed the special seats and a rolling dolly contraption that assisted in the raising of the seats.

"The dolly moved in front, picking up one section at a time," Smith said. "There was a place to fasten the seats and it left the whole floor wide open.

"The seats were built by Jean Verchefsky at his shop in South Venice."

The special seats were an important part of the arena because, in addition to using the building for rehearsals and preview shows, there were plans to hold home shows, ice skating shows, conventions and athletic events there. The first preview performance of the circus was held at the new arena in 1962.

Venetians seemed as excited about the arrival of the show as had the city fathers who had cut the deal. When the circus arrived in town for the very first time, more than 10,000 people turned out to see it arrive at the train depot and march to its new winter quarters.

Circus manager Concello had done much to save the circus. The move to Venice and the restriction of circus bookings primarily to arenas and auditoriums was part of the overall reorganization plan.

Without having to concern itself with the railroad business, the lodging and restaurant industries, the circus would finally be able to concentrate only on its main business — show business.

The circus was expected to boost the economy of

Photo courtesy of Larry Kellogg
Elephants practice their routine in this 1971 photo depicting a rehearsal at the Venice Circus Arena, shown in the background. Still in place in 2004, as this book was being printed, were the heavy iron rings used to tether the elephants in place between rehearsals and shows.

Venice by employing residents and by getting the name of the city into the national press, thereby luring more visitors and their tourist dollars to the city.

What was needed next was another P.T. Barnum. But at least The Greatest Show on Earth was alive and kicking, touring the country and adjusting to its new organization and to its new venues.

Timing is everything, and by 1968 the time was right for a latter-day P.T. Barnum to take the show to the next

Rehearsal time in the early days of the Venice Circus Arena, which was designed to duplicate the show floor of Madison Square Garden, where the circus played its longest run.

level. He arrived, in the form of Irvin Feld, the Barnum of the 20th century.

Actually he had been there for nearly 10 years, giving advice on the new arena venues while acting as an independent promoter and booking agent. While the circus managers learned from Feld, Feld learned from them too, eventually acquiring large doses of sawdust in his blood.

In 1966, while Lloyd Morgan went to Europe to be trainmaster of the Ringling unit there, Charlie Smith became trainmaster of the American unit of The

Greatest Show on Earth. One year later, as Smith dealt with a train that had grown from 15 cars to 40 cars, the Ringling family gave up majority ownership of the circus that bore its name, selling control of the circus to the

Photo courtesy of the Venice Archives and Area Historical Collection

Workers set up equipment in the Ringling Bros. and Barnum & Bailey Circus Arena in Venice prior to a preview show in the 1960s. Circus fans filled the 5,000-seat building at every preview show before the circus took off on its annual tour after six-eight weeks of rehearsals. In the 1980s, the length of the Venice rehearsal time was shortened and preview shows were given in early January rather than late February.

Hoffeld Corp. Its principals were Irvin and Israel Feld and Judge Roy Hofheinz, but Irvin Feld was the leader.

Feld wasted no time.

He spent money to make money. He created a second touring company, the Red Unit, to handle extra show dates. The original unit would be called the Blue Unit.

The Red Unit featured legendary animal trainer Gunther Gebel-Williams. Smith was designated as the Red Unit's trainmaster and Morgan was brought back to the United States to become general manager of the new Blue Unit.

Feld turned things around in four years, selling the huge show to toy giant Mattel in 1971, but staying on as the show's manager. Feld and his son, Kenneth, who became his business partner the day after graduation from Boston University, bought the circus back in 1982. Feld Entertainment has been in charge ever since.

Riding the rails again

While Feld promoted the show, Smith moved it, using his expertise to place coaches, flat cars and the two tunnel cars in such a way that the 40-car train could move as one unit and as easily as it had when there were just 15 cars. The cars' placement determined how the train would be loaded and unloaded.

Smith had learned much under Morgan and was particularly adept at speaking the language of the railroad with engineers and crewmen. That skill kept the train on schedule so that the circus never missed a performance in the 16 years that Smith was in charge.

It did miss one show a few years before Smith became trainmaster, he said. It was in 1965, the year Smith married Kitty, his second wife.

A derailment caused by a broken wheel occurred as

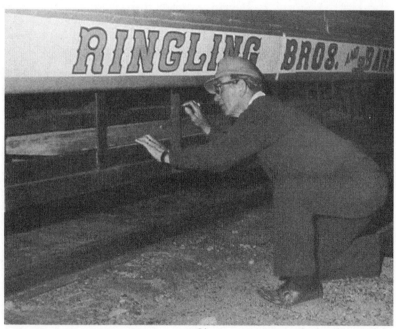

Photo courtesy of Charlie Smith

Ringling Bros. and Barnum & Bailey Circus trainmaster Charlie Smith checks to make sure that ramps are loaded properly before moving the circus train out of town.

the train was heading into Cleveland.

"People came and watched the rigging being set up," Smith said. "There was no show that night but only six people asked for refunds."

The show played the old Cleveland Arena at 3900 Prospect Ave. The Shrine Circus had the contract for the larger Public Auditorium in downtown Cleveland.

"That was one tough building to get into," Smith

Photo courtesy of Charlie Smith

Ringling trainmaster Charlie Smith drives a Clark to unload a circus wagon from the train. When Smith was inducted in the Sarasota Circus Ring of Fame in 2004, Tim Holman said that "all of Smith's innovations are still in use today on all the Ringling shows."

said of the arena. "There was a 90-degree turn into the arena. I had to build a set of dollies to get the rubber wagon into the arena. The animals had to be kept in tents in the parking lot."

Kitty worked as a wardrobe mistress in the show, replacing sequins, helping dress performers and fixing zippers. The couple traveled in their own compartment on the train.

Although the job of trainmaster is a management or executive-level job, it also can be a dirty job, especially for someone like Smith, who really got into his work, becoming a self-trained mechanical engineer and railroad expert. By talking "railroad," and mentioning such things as switching and cuts in the train, other trainmen knew that he knew his job and respected him.

His years of circus building came in handy as he perfected the potentially dangerous art of loading and unloading flat cars. With his six-man crew, Smith would set the runs at the end of the flat car and unload the wagons for the transportation manager to deliver to the arena and back when the show was ready to move on.

To accelerate the loading and unloading process, Smith devised a two-wheel poling dolly that facilitated pulling the wagon down the flat cars.

Eventually truck tractors accelerated the process

Photo by Kim Cool

This plaque is located on the northeast quadrant of St. Armand's Circle, Sarasota. Inscribed in bronze:

CHARLIE SMITH

In a remarkable 60-year career, he served stints as a performer, musician, pie car operator, boss canvasman, transportation superintendent and as trainmaster of one of the twentieth century's greatest traveling circuses. For 16 years, he directed the complex movements of Ringling Brothers and Barnum & Bailey's mile-long train over more than 300,000 miles without the show missing a single performance.

Tom Dillon, Tim Holan, Peggy Williams

93

even more.

Smith and his crew also were responsible for train maintenance. To that end they checked brake shoes and discs while carefully going over all the rolling stock to keep it in good repair. Even though it had been a long time since Smith had been hired as a welder by Art Concello, the trainmaster's experience and knowledge of welding, painting and carpentry continued to come in handy even when he had risen to the top as the train master of The Greatest Show on Earth.

Years after his retirement, circus stars such as the world-famous aerialist Tito Gaona would speak in glowing terms of Smith.

"He always asked if we had enough water," Gaona said. "And he would make sure our air conditioning was working."

The trainmaster also had to be a bit of a math wizard, fitting the right number of 16- to-20-foot wagons on each 96-foot long flat car, while also keeping track of the kind of wagons involved.

Wagons were numbered according to their content: one series of numbers for wardrobe wagons, another for props or ring curbing.

Smith remained in the job of trainmaster until 1981, when he retired for the first time but was soon brought

Photo by Kim Cool

Ringling Bros. and Barnum & Bailey Circus trainmaster Charlie Smith is proud of this bronze statue made especially for him by Venice area artist Ann Fleming Copeland in 2002.

back to work to help refurbish and recycle train cars in the Venice yard.

In 1977, Smith received one of the greatest honors in the circus field when the Illinois-based Circus Fans of America chartered the Charlie Smith Tent.

Still one of the organization's most active tents, its members are all die-hard Smith fans. Many came to his induction into the Sarasota Ring of Fame in 2004.

Red and Blue

Offsetting the costs of the second unit, were the cost savings accruing to the circus because a new show could now run for two years and play to twice as many people. In a plan that Feld Enterprises would also use in its ice skating shows some years later, Feld would use the basic format of a show for two years.

The 134th Edition of The Greatest Show on Earth's blue unit debuted in Tampa in 2004. The Red Unit — the 133rd Edition — was due to return to winter quarters in Tampa to debut early in 2005 as the 135th Edition. The explanation was offered by circus publicist Larry Kellogg.

"The Red Unit debuts in odd years," Kellogg said. "The Blue Unit debuts in even years."

(A third edition — the Gold Unit — debuted in

Photo by Kim Cool

Art Concello's granddaughter, Antoinette Concello, and her son, Shawn Concello, 5. The medal was given to her father, Randall Concello, during the 2004 Sarasota Circus Ring of Fame induction ceremony. Moments later, he left the grandstand to give the medal to his grandson, Shawn.

97

Rome, Ga. on March 6, 2004.)

The first edition of the Red Unit hit the road in 1969, with the legendary Gunther Gebel-Williams as its star. Irvin Feld had selected him especially for the new unit.

Headlining the Blue Unit was another famous animal trainer, Charlie Baumann.

Smith's wife, Kitty, joined the circus's wardrobe department shortly after their 1965 marriage. While Smith knew every inch of the mechanical aspect of the great show, she soon learned every inch of the performers as she fitted, stitched and repaired their costumes.

Now retired, the Smiths maintain a home in Nokomis, just a few miles north of the Venice train depot and arena. They still receive annual invitations to attend dress rehearsals of the shows.

Smith, with the late Art Concello, who was a trapeze performer before he ran the circus, was inducted into the Circus Ring of Fame on St. Armands Circle in Sarasota, Jan. 17, 2004. Also honored that day were aerialist Galla Shawn and the Konyot family of equestriennes. Honored in earlier years were giants of the circus such as Gebel-Williams, the Bale family of Venice, the five Ringling Brothers, clowns Otto Greibling and Lou Jacobs and others.

Founded in 1988 to recognize those who have made

significant contributions to the circus, the Ring of Fame had honored 74 individuals and groups by 2004, including the five Ringling Brothers who were honored together on one plaque. A bronze bust of John Ringling marks the circle on the north side.

Concello did much to save the Ringling show during one of its most trying times. He had to deal with both financial and labor problems while the show was transformed from a tent show to an arena show. Experience as a flying trapeze artist and the owner of several circuses contributed to the expertise he brought to his final circus job.

Greibling and Jacobs were two of the four master clowns named by Ringling. They also were instructors at Clown College, which Feld established in Venice in 1968. The one-of-a-kind school would bring the sleepy little beach town fame even as it filled a void in the circus. Within two years of its founding, a graduate from the first class, Frosty Little, would be well on his way to joining his mentors, Greibling and Jacobs, as a master clown.

Money begets money, and clowns were about to beget more clowns.

Fully recovered from its limp, the Ringling Bros. and Barnum & Bailey Circus was about to take Venice and the world by storm.

Kim Cool

Sue "Shammie" Kowalski with Irv "Amtrak" Armbruster
and Scrappy the clown at the dedication of the restored
Venice Train Depot on Oct. 24, 2004. These three clowns,
with Venice circus celebrities such as the late Gunther
Gebel-Williams, mounted a grass-roots campaign to keep
the circus in Venice when rumors first surfaced in the mid-
1980s that the circus was planning to leave Venice.

Part Two

Circus Days in Venice

Moving Day

The deal to move the circus to Venice had been struck at Christmas in 1959, but Venetians had to wait until the following Thanksgiving to see what the present contained.

Moving Day was Nov. 29, 1960. Most merchants closed their stores that day. There would be little business because everyone in town and a few thousand visitors were gathered at the Seaboard Airline Railroad Depot early in the morning. Those not at the depot lined the roads between there and the still-unfinished arena.

Students were excused from the local elementary school and many older children played hooky in order to be part of the historic occasion. Whether or not they realized that it was a historic occasion did not matter at the time.

"It was the greatest welcome ever afforded any organization in the history of the city," proclaimed a story in *Banner Line*, a circus publication of the time.

When the 15-car train pulled into the station 10 minutes early, at 8:50 a.m., it was said in the newspapers that the crowd's cheering could be heard blocks away.

All the city officials were there, armed with carefully prepared speeches in honor of this milestone day in the history of the city.

Also there were members and representatives of organizations such as the VFW and two carloads of chamber of commerce members.

While the circus folks heard the cheers, they did not hear the speeches. There was work to be done. No sooner had the train come to a stop than the circus manager, wardrobe man and others were scurrying about to unload the train cars and move into the new winter quarters.

Rudy Bundy, the show's treasurer at the time; Galla Shawn, the number one aerialist that year; and the show's personnel director were the only three members of the circus to stop to shake hands with the politicos and pose for a few photos with high school band members. (Galla Shawn was known for her head, balancing act on the trapeze. The climax of her act was to spin on her head on a second trapeze as it was lowered to the ground. She was inducted into the Sarasota Circus Ring of Fame in 2004, with Art Concello, Charlie Smith and equestrians Arthur, Alexander and Dorita Konyot.)

An impromptu band concert more than made up for the wasted speeches, especially when circus bandmaster Merle Evans stepped into the band's trumpet section.

As he cut loose with his cornet, "old timers recognized it as circus music that is circus music," the *Banner Line* writer wrote.

The Venice Area Chamber of Commerce president, Bud Wimmers, was ecstatic that day, for he was the one who set in motion the scenario that led to the Ringling circus's move to Venice.

Also on hand that day was George Browne, then 84. He had retired from the show in 1945, having served as an advance man, canvas man and more.

Browne had lived through thousands of 4 a.m. arrivals in cities around the country, had helped with unloading and had raised tents as often as he had put up banners announcing the arrival of "The Greatest Show on Earth."

On Nov. 29, the unloading was happening well after sunrise and before some 10,000 enthusiastic viewers who were being treated to what, for most people, is a once-in-a-lifetime opportunity — to see the circus unload its eight double-coach tunnel cars.

"As fast as one tractor brought out a string of compact wagons, another backed up to the ramp and hitched onto another string with no lost motion," *Banner Line's* reporter wrote.

Missing were all the clowns. According to an article in the *Venice Gondolier Sun*, the clowns were all with their families — in Sarasota. This was the beginning of the annual winter vacation and many of the clowns had not seen their families all year. As it was the first year in Venice, few if any of the performers had moved to the new city. Technically they were on vacation until Jan. 5 so most were doing just that — vacationing.

As soon as the unloading was finished and the animals cared for, trainers and grooms also would have lighter duties until rehearsals would begin.

Years later, in 2002, when archeologists were conducting a dig on the grounds of the old Venice Depot prior to its renovation, I met and spoke with several observers, some of whom had been around to witness one or more arrivals of the circus into Venice.

Nearly 50 years had gone by yet they remembered the train's arrival and unloading as if it were yesterday, so great an impact did the occasion make on the viewers.

They stayed to watch the diggers in hopes that some memento of the circus years would surface. None did.

Or was the glint in the eye of one man who spoke so eloquently about the train's arrival and the parade of the animals to the circus arena, memento enough? Just being at the old depot seemed to remove the years from his body, even as his story brought that time forward to those of us who were not in Venice on that special day in 1960. As he continued speaking, we could almost see the elephants, the zebra, the llama, donkeys, ponies and horses as they were taken from the train and lined up for the parade to the winter quarters site.

The Intracoastal Waterway did not yet exist in Venice so the parade simply headed west on Venice Avenue and south on the Tamiami Trail toward the airport. It would be seven years before the waterway would make an island of Venice.

And, it would be nearly two months before the circus arena would be finished and ready for rehearsals. Until then, the new winter quarters were not just smaller than the Sarasota winter quarters, but also confusing because it was still under construction.

Circus employees had to make do.

Their years of setting up camps all over the country paid off. By nightfall, they had erected a tent for some of the animals and had tethered the elephants nearby. The tigers and one lion were bedded down in one corner of the still-unfinished circus arena, ready to spend their first night in Venice.

Five weeks later, the circus was ready to give its first preview show in its new arena — a benefit for New College in Sarasota. Tickets were priced at $25-$1,000 per person, but the first five tickets sold actually brought in $5,000 per ticket, a tidy sum in those days.

Succeeding shows were open to the general public with tickets priced at $1.50-$3.50 per person.

During the first few years in Venice, a pattern developed. The show generally arrived in Venice about the first of December. Performers enjoyed four weeks off with their families during the holidays and then two weeks of daily rehearsals before the show would go out on the road for another season, but not before being blessed by the local priest, the Right Rev. Msgr. George Cummins of the Venice Church of the Epiphany (now the Epiphany Cathedral) with help from local altar boys.

Kim Cool

Big Top burns

For the second time in its history, the famed "Big Top" went up in flames. Unlike the tragic fire that claimed 167 lives in 1944, this fire, at the Venice winter quarters in 1962, destroyed only wagons and equipment.

Sadly, those wagons contained the last big tent used by Ringling and the wagons themselvews were historic, dating to 1936, when they had last been used to transport items for the show.

The old wagons had been destined to be used in a proposed "Ringlingland" circus theme park that had been proposed as an adjunct to the Venice winter quarters, It would have been built on land optioned by the circus when it signed its first lease with the city of Venice.

As reported in the *Sarasota Herald Tribune* March 20, that year, the fire was said to have accidentaally been started by a spark from a torch used to dismantle an old metal bleacher wagon. When the spark hit dry grass beneath the wagon, the fire erupted and soon engulfed the wagons, becoming hotter when the wagon's solid rubber tires became involved. One piece of the big tent was saved but the loss of the tent alone was estimated at $25,000, reporter Jack Briggs wrote. The fire may have been one of the major reasons that the proposed theme park was never built in Venice.

More likely is the fact that in those early days in

Photo by Kim Cool

Performers and animals would enter the Venice Circus Arena through this back hallway. Offices and dressing rooms were on either side. The Charlie Smith-designed seating was still in place in January 2004.

Venice, the circus was still recovering from its conversion from tent show to arena show.

Circus historian Richard J. EReynolds III, writing in *Bandwagon's* December 1994 edition, referred to "the dark days of its depression in the late 1950s and early 1960s," before the show's renaissance in Venice.

In the *Ringling Route Book*, (the first one printed since 1955) printed for the 1964 season, the Venice quarters were described as the "best in all history."

For the first time, the circus was occupying brand-new buildings "constructed exclusively for the needs of the circus."

By 1965, the train had grown to 25 cars, still a far cry from the days when the show traveled in four 25-car trains, but nearly double the number of cars that arrived in Venice five years earlier when the show was more a truck show than a train show.

In as many more years, the train would be nearly three-quarters of a mile long.

But things were turning around. The *Venice Gondolier Sun* that year pulished a circus souvenir section of its Jan. 7 edition and Venice author Walter Farley wrote "Little Black Goes to the Circus." It was the story of a circus pony by the man who had become famous for his Black Stallion books for older children.

Charly Bauman was pictured walking his tiger and the Bale family were pictured. The Bales were inducted into the Sarasota Ring of Fame in 2003 and continue to reside in Venice.

Photo by Kim Cool

The Bale family was collectively honored for its 350 years in the circus at the 2003 Sarasota Ring of Fame ceremony.

Kim Cool

With circus roots going back 350 years, the Bales attained stardom as trapezists and animal trainers. Like many of the great circus families, the Bales were a multi-talented group.

Daughter Gloria did trapeze, trick cycling, bareback riding and whatever was needed in the Ringling's big production numbers. Youngest sibling, Nbonnie, was on stage when just seven days old, in an elephant act with her father, Trevor Bale.

Dawnita did trapeze and her twin brother Elvin had a 25-year career as the most famous circus daredevil. He performed in the show's center ring for 15 years, doing heel catches on a trapeze, balancing on a highwire on a motorcycle and performing the Wheel of Death. Tragedy struck in 1987 when, while performing a human cannonball trick, he overshot his target and was permanently paralyzed from the waist down.

With acts such as the Bales and Bauman, and new winter quarters, things were looking up for the Ringling show. Promotor Irvin Feld had been wielding his magic in promoting the circus.

In 1967, he became its president.

One year later, Clown College would be opened in Venice and two years later The Greatest Show on Earth would celebrate its 100th birthday.

It was time to bring in some more really big acts. The circus was back on its feet and Feld was going to show the world that the 100-year-old show was more than just young at heart.

Like John Ringling and John Ringling North, Feld spared no expense to travel the world in search of the best and he found them, right up to and including the late and now legendary Gunther Gebel-Williams.

Gebel-Williams was discovered in Germany in 1968 at the suggestion of Victor Gaona, patriarch of the world-famous Flying Gaonas. Feld was so impressed with the young animal trainer that he bought the entire Circus Williams in order to gain Gunther.

To this day, memories center around the arrival of The Greatest Show on Earth after its annual tour, especially the animals, led by the handsome young trainer.

"I can remember the parade," resident Vonni Fagan said. "They would parade down Venice Avenue and you were so close to the elephants you could almost touch them."

Fagan said that in November the circus train would pull into the Venice train station and the elephants would be unloaded there before parading over the bridge on Venice Avenue and then along Tamiami Trail to the Ringling Bros. and Barnum & Bailey Circus Arena (Venice Arena) on Avenue del Circo.

Photo courtesy of Sigrid Gebel

With the Venice arena in the background, a young
Gunther Gebel-Williams takes a break from teaching the
elephants their new act for the following season. As this
book went to press a statue of the animal trainer was
being prepared to be erected at the site of the old Venice
Train Depot, where he unloaded so many circus animals
over the years before countless fans.

Hundreds more residents have shared similar memories over the past few years.

Most often they spoke of the animals and Gunther Gebel-Williams, who became Venice's favorite son during his life there.

Gunther and his wife Sigrid had met in Berlin where both were performing with the Circus Williams, source of the second part of his hyphenated name. Married, with daughter Tina, they came to America in 1968, eventually settling in Venice.

Gebel-Williams worked with all animals: lions and tigers and elephants and giraffes and zebras, often combining animals in a single number even though those animals were natural enemies. One act he performed with 20 leopards, three black panthers and mountian lions, all in the same ring, Sigrid said. In another act, never performed by any other trainer since his retirement, Gebel-Williams "had a tiger on the back of an elephant and another tiger on the backs of two horses," she said.

During the season, the family traveled in their own private rail car on the circus train, living the good life with most everything they needed.

Except for an education for their children. Tina spent one brief period of time at Venice Elementary School before being sent to live with family friends in North Carolina during the school year because there was no school on the circus train in those days. Then, when Mark Oliver was born, Sigrid said she could not bear to have both children away at school so she petitioned Kenneth Feld to start a school for the children of circus performers and workers. It was in the mid 1970s.

"I found Bob Grote," she said."He is now in New York City with Notre Dame. In an interview for a newspaper, he told the reporter that he 'ran with the circus to join a school,' " Sigrid said.

WIth the family reunited on the show, mother and dauther did a Liberty horse act and worked in the elephant act orchestrated by Gunther. Son Mark Oliver joined in as soon as he was big enough to walk.

Their life was the circus and the cities where the show played. They loved arriving at Madison Square Garden but after the 10-week run there, Guther could not wait to get to Philadelphia, where he could give the animals some fresh air after their 10 weeks of being cooped up inside the Garden, Sigrid said.

Venice also was special.

"It was such a thrill for us to see our fellow Venetians sitting in lines to buy tickets despite the heat," she said. "When Gunther was practicing, people would walk down to the arena and start watching. The tigers were concentrat-

RINGLING BROS and BARNUM & BAILEY

CIRCUS SCHOOL

Student's Name *Mark Oliver Gebel*

Grade *3rd - 4th*

Season *1979*

S·bject	I	II	III	IV	V
Matnematics	A	A	A	A	B+
Reading	B	A	A	A	A
Gra··mar	A	A	B	B	B
Spelling	A	A	A	A	A
Composition	A	A	B+	A	A
Handwriting	B+	A	A	A	A
Socia¹ Studies	B	A	A	A	B+
Drawing	A	A	A	A	A
Neatness	B+	A	A	A	?
Conduct	—	—	—	—	—
Effort	A	A	A	A	A

Courtesy of Sigrid Gebel

Circus School report card of Mark Oliver Gebel, 1979.

117

ing on what they were doing and Gunther didn't mind the watchers."

Like any other resident, Gebel-Williams and his family would have to wait their turn at local restaurants, often chit-chatting with others in line, neighbor to neighbor.

Peggi Paquette, a teacher at theLaurel Nokomis School and long-time circus fan, is one in a long list of fans of the late animal trainer. When he died July 19, 2001, after a year-long bout with brain cancer, more than 2,000 mourners packed Our Lady of Lourdes Church in Venice for the memorial service.

Flowers and other tributes were sent from all over the world. Sigfried and Roy send white orchids in a Waterford crystal bowl — the orchids symbolic of their own white tigers. The Hagenbach and Wallace costume company sent a tiger cub all made of fresh flowers. The Ringling circus sent a floral wagon wheel with a broken spoke, symbolizing the death of the star. Barbara Mandrell and countless celebrities flew into Venice to take their place side by side with the rest of us who were simply fans. I was there to cover the funeral for the *Venice Gondolier Sun,* and the next day I was in the Gebel home chatting with his widow about the remarkable man she had married more than 30 years earlier when both were performing in Europe. For three consecutive issues, the twice-weekly paper had extensive coverage of the home town hero.

"His public legacy is secure," said Kenneth Feld, Feld Entertainment CEO and close personal friend of Gebel-Williams. "He took animal training from whips and chairs to mutual respect. He changed the American circus forever."

Photo courtesy of Sigrid Gebel

A young Gunther Gebel-Williams gets up close and personal with a "smiling" black panther while preparing for his debut year with The Greatest Show on Earth during the 1969 season. Circus president Irvin Feld created a second unit of the circus especially for the young star from Europe.

Photo courtesy of Sigrid Gebel

A hard-working tiger works with famous animal trainer Gunther Gebel-Williams in the tiger cage on the back lot of the Venice circus arena in the days when The Greatest Show on Earth wintered in Venice, Fla.

While mourners gathered at the church, Gebel-Williams made one final appearance in the center ring at the Venice Circus Arena where he had rehearsed his animals for the first time in America in 1968. The arena was almost new then and the animal trainer was barely into his 20s.

At the time of his final appearance on July 24, 2001, brought there in the antique golden hearse owned by the Farley Funeral Home of Venice, the old arena had become a white elephant, filled with nothing but memories and possibly a few ghosts.

The final visit had been secretly planned by Sigrid, and only the driver of the hearse and David Farley knew that plan, she said the following day while we chatted in her dining room. The casket was carried into the center ring, draped in his purple performance cape. A lone spotlight illuminated the setting as the immediate family and closest friends from the funeral cortege gathered for a private prayer before the public service at the church.

Planned to the last detail by Sigrid, the funeral was an extraordinary event befitting an extraordinary man. It was presided over by Father Jerry Hogan, the circus priest. Tenor Eric Michael Gillette took a day's leave from Broadway, where he was appearing as Ralph in "Kiss Me Kate." Gillette had been the ringmaster of The Greatest

Show on Earth during the last 10 years of Gebel-Williams'
30-year run. He had lived in Venice from 1987 to 89, witnessing the creation of Gebel-Williams' farewell tour with
the circus.

"He knew what was going on in everyone's life in the
show," Gillette said after the funeral. "If anyone needed
anything, he was there for us, and he had a work ethic like
no other."

Sigrid spoke of his work ethic too.

Photo courtesy of Sigrid Gebel

**Gunther Gebel-Williams with his wife Sigrid and children
Tina and Mark Oliver. Photo was taken in the early 1980s.**

"He needed to work and so did the animals," she said. "Once you have animals it is a life-long commitment."

In the pristine Jacaranda neighborhood where the Gebels live, neighbors tend to take good care of their yards. On the rare occasion when they might slip up, Gunther would help out, pulling a weed that was unnoticed or sweeping up leaves that had been overlooked. He did this even during the last year of his life. He also worked with his young grandson Marcus, showing the 3-year-old how to create an animal act, using a miniature circus ring and toy animals. Sigrid showed me a treasured photo of that day, one of the last good days the star would enjoy.

On another day, he went fishing with an out-of-town visitor, Dr. Richard Houck, emeritus veterinarian for the Ringling circus. Houck last saw his friend July 12, 2001, one week before the animal trainer's death.

"The next Thursday I was in the mountains," Houck said at the funeral. "When I looked up and saw an eagle circle above, I knew he was gone."

Gebel-Williams had died that morning in Venice.

At his funeral a video was shown of Gebel-Williams in his work clothes, carrying his broom, shovel and pail into the elephant barn. Other scenes showed the star in his performance clothes with the flowing cape and the glittery decorations. His stunning blond hair and infectious smile were his trademarks. He met and worked with some of the greatest entertainers of all time but most of all he loved his family and his animals and his adopted home —Venice.

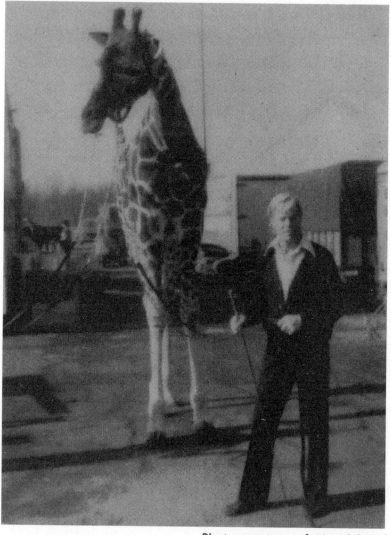

Photo courtesy of Sigrid Gebel
Gunther Gebel-Williams unloading a giraffe.

Photo courtesy of Sigrid Gebel

One of the last portraits of the famous animal trainer, Gunther Gebel-Williams, was taken in 2000. In the back row are his son, Mark Oliver Gebel, and Mark's wife, Christina Moraru, daughter, Tina Gebel DelMoral and her husband, Edward DelMoral. In the center is Lorenzo Delmoral. Gunther Gebel-Williams is seated at left with his wife Sigrid Gebel and their grandson Marcus, the youngest child of Tina and Edward.

Sigrid shared the glamor with him and his fans. When he became ill, she shared his pain and cared for him at home where he died surrounded by his family. During that time, she shielded him and his fans.

After his death, she shared the most precious mementoes. His shovel was presented to Louis Pierre, an animal caretaker who had come to America with Gebel-Williams. His broom was given to Pete Cimini, a young animal caretaker who was like a son to the famous star. His famous purple cape was given to Lorenzo DelMoral, son of Edward DelMoral, husband of Tina Gebel. His cowboy hat was bequethed to his grandson Marcus DelMoral and his silver belt buckle to Hunter William Gebel, son of Mark Oliver Gebel.

All that was missing from the last act of the greatest animal trainer of all time was one more standing ovation. He got that at the end of his funeral service in Venice, the city that loved him as much as he loved it.

He is buried at Venice Memorial Gardens in a plot marked with a simple but elegant bronze plaque — a fitting tribute.

Another tribute was planned soon after his death — a bronze statue of the star in his flowing cape and in the pose he often struck atop an elephant while making his entrance into the circus arena. The train depot was selected because that is where the animals were unloaded from the train in the early days in Venice.

As this book went to press, the statue was nearing completion by sculptor Edward Kasprowitz, in Apollo Beach.

During more than a quarter of a century with The Greatest Show on Earth, Gebel-Williams had entertained more than 200 million people. He had never missed one of more than 12,000 performances in America, a record that may never be matched let alone broken.

He had endeared himself to both neighbors and fans. He will be remembered as a great showman but even more for the lessons he taught — that humans and animals could work together.

He changed the American circus forever.

Known as the Greatest Animal Trainer of All Time, Gebel-Williams was nearly as well known for the American Express commercial he made with his favorite leopard, Kenny, draped around his neck. He also was a featured performer on several television specials and a regular guest on some of the top TV shows of his era, including Johnny Carson's "Tonight Show."

It is not surprising that so many Venetians frequented the circus arena when he was in town preparing for the next season. They hoped to get a glimpse of their favorite son and his animals.

Although the Venice circus grounds were not open to the public as the Sarasota site had been, two areas were in full view of passersby on the Tamiami Trail — the practice ring for elephants and the temporary cage for training lions and tigers.

A large tent housing the elephants was erected just west of the elephants' practice ring. The cat-training cage was west of that tent, a short distance from the 55,000-square-foot arena. Just north of the arena was a tent housing horses. A canvas tent top over several wagons placed south of the arena was used for offices. The gorillas were kept in two air-conditioned cages just south of the office area. Several wagons used in the days

Photo by Kim Cool

The old Venice circus arena, once the winter home of The Greatest Show on Earth, outlived its usefulness and was too costly to renovate.

before the show put away its big top were at the south
end of the circus property. Another outdoor training ring
was just west of those wagons.

Gunther's building

Between the arena and the cat cages was a round
building, about 60-feet in diameter, housing a 45-foot-
round circus ring. Its peaked metal roof offered plenty of
headroom for a variety of acts. It was frequently used by

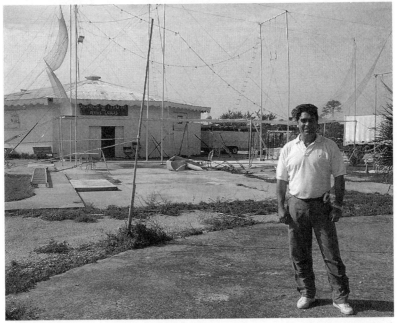

Photo by Kim Cool

**Tito Gaona stands before the little building he hoped to
turn into the Venice Museum of Circus Arts. Behind him
is the rigging used by him for his trapeze school.**

129

Gebel-Williams and his animals, his friend and fellow circus star, Tito Gaona said.

By 2004, that little building was the only former cir-

Photo courtesy of Tito Gaona

Tito Gaona, after rebounding to the catcher's trapeze during a performance in 1978, with the Ringling Bros. and Barnum & Bailey Circus.

cus building still in use. It has been leased from the city of Venice since 2000 by Gaona, a former Ringling trapeze star for his aerial school, one of several he operates in the United States.

"I want to save that building," Gaona said. "I want to do a circus museum there."

To that end, Gaona created a 501(c)(3) corporation, the Venice Circus Arts Foundation Inc.

"Many of the Venice residents remember the excitement of watching the elephants march through town on their way to the circus train, which was parked at the Venice tain depot," he said. "Every winter the circus came to town, bringing color and excitement to this small city on the gulf. The most famous acts in the world called the Venice Arena home."

In addition to Gaona and his family's act, the Flying Gaonas, the most honored clowns in the world (Lou Jacobs, Otto Greibling and Frosty Little); the most famous animal trainer in the world (Gunther Gebel-Williams and hundreds of other circus performers made Venice their home. Some, like Little, lived in Venice only those weeks or months when they had to be in town to prepare for the next show. Little was here a bit more than that as he taught at Clown College for many years, arriving in Venice nearly three months before the show returned. Others, like Gaona and

Photo courtesy of Tito Gaona

While riding the rails from town to town with the circus, Tito Gaona could enjoy a game of chess with a friend in his private quarters aboard the Ringling train. Animal trainer Charly Bauman's quarters were in the other half of the car, at the end of the train.

Photo courtesy of Tito Gaona

Tito Gaona enjoyed all the comforts of home in his private quarters on the Ringling Bros. and Barnum & Bailey Circus train, often staying on the train even when in his hometown of Venice. He had a living room, kitchen, dining room, washer and dryer, "big bathroom with a shower," a guest room for his brothers, and a lot of windows.

Gebel-Williams, maintained year-round homes in Venice.

Gaona actually grew up in Venice, living there part of the year and the remainder of the year in Mexico.

"I traveled with my dad in the summer," he said. "I got into the family trampoline act and was on the Ed Sullivan Show."

By the time he was 12, in 1959, he had performed his first triple somersault on the trapeze, the youngest person to accomplish that trick. He went on to set the record for consecutive triples, performing in 675 shows per year, including three shows every Saturday, during his 19 year-career with the Ringling Bros. and Barnum & Bailey Circus.

Gaona's parents bought his present home in Venice in 1964, the same year his youngest brother, Marco, was born at Venice Hospital. The home's prior owner had been Mark Leddy, a talent scout for Sullivan. With a grass-covered side yard large enough for the trapeze rigging and enough room to expand the house from three bedrooms to six, the house was perfect for the family. While many Venetians watched the family practice in the side yard, John Ringling North must never have driven down that road, which was only a mile from the Venice Circus Arena.

Despite his Venice roots, Gaona was "discovered" in Europe. While performing in Goteborg, Sweden, the Gaonas received a radiogram from John Ringling North. It said that he was sending Trolle Rhodin to look at their act.

Circus Days in Sarasota & Venice

It was just days after the family had signed a contract to perform with the Tower Circus in Blackpool, England.

Committed to Tower, the Gaonas were disappointed, especially young Tito, who wanted North to see his triple. The family had wanted to be in the Ringling show but Concello, as the director of the circus, had only been interested in the family's trampoline act.

"We lived barely a mile from the Ringling winter quarters in Venice," Tito Gaona said. "North himself could have auditioned us there six months earlier. Now he was sending an agent half way around the world to see us."

Figuring they had nothing to lose, the Gaonas performed for Rhodin, who almost immediately offered them a contract. Although feeling honor-bound to fulfill their Tower contract, when it turned out that it had not been correctly signed, Tito convinced his father to accept the Ringling offer. The Ringling show would pay the act nearly six figures, including private dressing rooms and a car on the silver circus train, if desired.

They would finish out their fall commitments in Europe and join The Greatest Show on Earth in Raleigh, N.C., on Feb. 15, 1966, right after its Venice debut.

And, they would be flying, with Victor as the catcher for his children, Chela, Tito and Armando. It was the beginning of a 19-year run that Tito would have with The

Photo courtesy of the Venice Archives and Area Historical Collection
Venice provided the perfect climate for the winter quarters of the Ringling Bros. and Barnum & Bailey Circus. During the annual winter hiatus, performers could stay in shape by practicing on equipment set up in their own yard. On Spadaro Road, the Flying Gaonas had a trapeze rig in the lot next to their house.

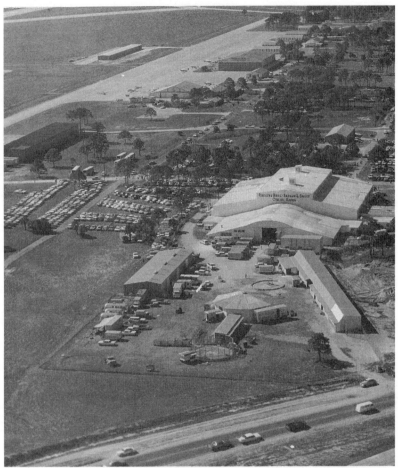

Photo courtesy of the Venice Archives and Area Historical Collection
In the early 1970s when this photo was taken, the circus was well established in its Venice winter quarters next to the airport. The little round building in the foreground is the building that Tito Gaona was hoping to save for conversion as a circus museum in Venice. In the ensuing years, the arena has outlived its usefiness and homes and businesses have filled in the vacant land to the right (north) of the airport. Public beaches and the Gulf of Mexico are just beyond the area shown at the top of the photo.

137

Greatest Show on Earth.

Like the other stars on the show, Gaona had his own private living quarters on the train.

"I shared a car with Charly Bauman," he said. "ours was the last car. No one could go through it."

Born Victor Daniel to a Spanish mother and Mexican father, Gaona was called "Tito" by his younger siblings who could not pronounce his given name. The nickname stayed. Gaona's father was the catcher for the Flying Gaonas when Tito was a youngster.

His father taught him to do the triple.

"Do it blindfolded," the father would say to the youngster. "Just feel it. You have to stop the turn. Count it in your mind and then open your eyes. That kept me on track."

The other thing that kept him on track was changing his act for every show. Working so closely together, everyone in the family knew the signals for each trick.

"The audience loved the rebound more than anything," Gaona said about the trick in which he would fall from the trapeze into the net and rebound to the trapeze. "They didn't care about the triple."

Forever young, Gaona looks at least 10 years younger than his true age, and can still do triples, he said.

Why does he do it?

"The breeze in your face as you're flying," he said.
"There is no life like it. I got paid to see the world."
Children in the circus spoke five languages, he said.
"It was like a little United Nations. The circus provided
an education that you cannot buy."

Gaona said that he learned a lot about people while
traveling all over the world and working with so many different people. But he always considered Venice his home,
even in his early days with the Ringling show when he
would remain on the train while in Venice.

"It was my home," he said. "Everything I needed was
there. I stayed there more than in my house, although I
used to practice more in the yard (at his house on Spadaro).

Like other Venice visitors and residents in those days, I
remember driving down that street and seeing the trapeze
and nets set up. Venice was the circus city in those days
and the sideyard trapeze setup was just one of the more
obvious clues.

Residents often would experience chance meetings with
performers such as Gaona and Gebel-Williams.

Both appeared in the centennial edition of The Greatest
Show on Earth, which debuted in the Venice Arena. As both
shows wintered in Venice from the second unit's inception
in 1969 until 1986, the debut of the centennial show was the
biggest show on earth in addition to being The Greatest
Show on Earth. As a Venice visitor that year, I was at the

world premier of the 100th anniversary edition in 1970. It was huge, lasting for nearly four hours.

With its purchase of the Circus Williams, the circus had experienced a giant growth spurt at an important moment in its history.

Among the featured acts in that 100th anniversary show was Jeanette Williams, the daughter of the late owner of Circus Williams. She was a 2004 honoree at Circus Celebrity Night at the John & Mable Ringling Museum of Art's Museum of the Circus.

In introducing Williams, awards presenter Steve Smith said, "As a baby clown of 19, I'd heard she was formidable, a tough lady, statuesque, a beautiful woman with a whip!"

Williams said "The Greatest Show on Earth" became

Photos courtesy of Jeanette Williams

Jeanette Williams made her debut in The Greatest Show on Earth at the age of 19, performing a Liberty Horse act with 24 white Lippizaner Stallions in one ring.

her mantra.

"Until there is commitment, there is hesitency," she said. "Boldness has genius, power and magic in it."

Living in the circus with her parents, Harry and Carolina, Williams learned every aspect of the circus. She began by training birds and dogs, then switched to liberty ponies before developing a Liberty horse act featuring 24 stallions in one ring. Multi-talented, she also handled the Circus Williams payroll and supervised costumes.

Joining the Ringling show in 1968, she worked as both an animal trainer and performer. In addition to the liberty acts, she created acts with elephants, ponies and tigers. As a performer, she was the first person to present uncaged cheetahs on horseback.

Today she is the owner of a theatrical agency, supplying talent for circuses, theme parks and others. She also has been recognized in several countries for her involvement with the protection and breeding of endangered species of animals.

"I started the first breeding programs for white tigers and white lions in Europe," she said. "I don't know any circus person who is not nice to animals. It is their bread and butter. My heart belongs to the circus and to the performers."

Also inducted with Williams that night was the late Otto Greibling. He too had been in that 100th anniversary

Photo courtesy of Jeanette Williams

**Jeanette Williams, performing with two cageless cheetahs
in The Greatest Show on Earth during the 1970s.**

143

show more than 30 years ago.

Like many a performer, Greibling had worked in a variety of acts, beginning with the Hodgini Riding Act. There are still Hodginis in the circus, and in Venice.

Greibling finally joined the Ringling show in 1951, becoming one of its top clowns and becoming known for his metal pie plate act. Later he became an instructor at Clown College.

Greibling lost his larynx to cancer in 1970. He continued clowning and teaching until his death in 1972. He was inducted into the Clown Hall of Fame in 1989.

In preceding years, honorees have included the Flying Gaonas (2003), the Bertini Family of acrobats (2002), animal trainer Charly Bauman (2001), aerialist Dolly Jacobs (1999), Gunther Gebel-Williams (1998), Lou Jacobs (1980), trainer and ringmaster John Herriott (1976) and others, many of whom still reside in the Venice and Sarasota areas.

The Ringling circus may be gone from Venice as it is from Sarasota, but its legacy will live forever in those two cities.

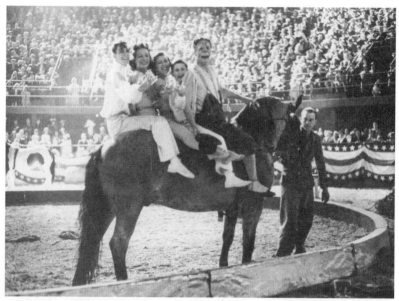

Photo courtesy of the Venice Archives and Area Historical Collection
The Hodgini Family Riding Act perform in the Ringling show.

Photo by Kim Cool
A miniature circus tent display at the Ringling Museum of the Circus in Sarasota.

Bring in the clowns

It was 1968, time for Venice to begin clowning around seriously.

Can a circus ever have enough clowns?

For The Greatest Show on Earth in the 1960s, having clowns at all was becoming a concern to owner Irvin Feld. Considering that a one-time clown named John Ringling was one of the great show's founders, it would not do to run out of clowns.

(The rare portrait of John Ringling as a clown is in the collection of circus memorabilia belonging to Robert

Horne of Sarasota.)

As the circus approached its 10-year anniversary at its winter quarters in Venice, all was not right with The Greatest Show on Earth.

Times were changing.

Running away to join the circus was not something children of the 1960s did.

Love beads, anti-war protests and hippies were the fashion in those early days of the Vietnam era. Children ran away to join a commune, not a circus.

The Greatest Show on Earth was down to just 14 clowns, a commodity referred to by the late P.T. Barnum as "the pegs on which to hang a circus."

The quickest way to succeed in any business is to identify a need and supply it.

Feld's solution to the diminishing supply of clowns was to open Clown College. If clowns were not swarming to the circus, the circus would train its own.

As the winter home of the Ringling show, Venice was gaining national and even international press. Clown College added yet another dimension to the city on the gulf.

Feld's college would safeguard the future of clowning in America and also dispel the notions of skeptics who felt that clowning was a God-given talent.

For three decades, despite the number of visiting snowbirds in search of Florida tans, each fall, white faces continued to be spotted around the town.

It was not unusual for a driver to pass a bicyclist, look in the rear view mirror and discover a clown face. I know, for I was one of those drivers.

Over on Miami Avenue, graduation photos appeared each November in the display windows of a local photography studio. The subjects were not clad in black drapes or dark suits but in colorful costumes, painted faces and outlandish hats and wigs.

Those graduates marched to the beat of a different drummer.

The normal graduation procession was replaced by a performance of the class clowns. Consider that at Clown College every student was a class clown.

Invitations were coveted for the graduation performance, which offered a chance to see a future Emmett Kelly, Lou Jacobs or Frosty Little.

In fact, those attending the first graduation in 1968 did see Frosty Little. After several years of clowning, Little's acceptance to and graduation from Clown College paved the way for his stardom with The Greatest Show on Earth and to his eventual selection as a master clown, one of just four clowns ever awarded

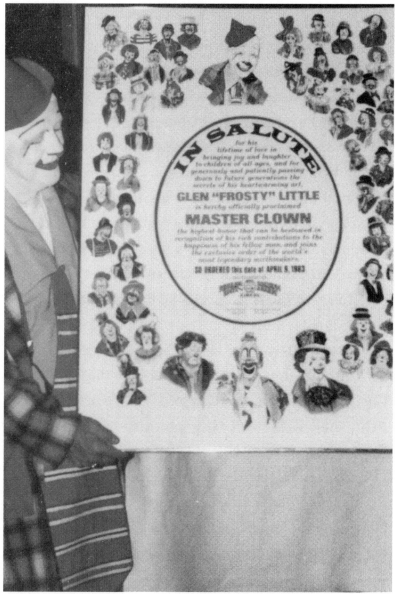

From the collection of Dixon Little

Frosty Little, a member of the first class of Clown College, was named a Master Clown on April 1, 1983, by Irvin Feld.

that honor.

Little was 42 when he entered that first class at
Clown College, possibly one of the oldest students to
ever attend the celebrated school. In most classes, the
average age was closer to 20, but Little quickly made up
for lost time, becoming Boss Clown on the Red Unit
within two years of his graduation and Director of
Clowns for the Red and Blue Units 10 years after that.
He supervised 75 clowns in the two shows, helped
develop new acts and annually spent a few months in
Venice as a teacher at his alma mater, Clown College.

"They put us (he and his wife Pat) in a house on
Center Road," Little said. "It always had a pool.

"I really enjoyed the show. It was so exciting."

The other three Master Clowns were the late Bobby
Kay, Otto Greibling and Lou Jacobs, all Sarasota residents, and all destined to be showered with honors for
their work.

Jacobs and Greibling have been honored at the
Ringling Museum of the Circus, Circus Celebrity
Nights; Jacobs in 1980 and Greibling in 2004. Greibling's
award was given posthumously as a great performer of
the Circus Past.

Greibling, born in 1896, began his career as an
apprentice bareback rider with the Hodgini Riding Act,

toured awhile with Tom Mix, and finally switching to clowning after suffering a bad fall. He joined the Ringling show in 1951, becoming known for several acts, including his "metal pie plate act."

In 1970, his larynx was removed because of cancer and he spent the last two years of his life miming for real instead of for fun as he had the previous 40 years of his career.

"I didn't know he didn't have a voice," said Clown College student Steve Smith. "He communicated that well. Everything he did was perfection. Bauman (Charly Bauman — the animal trainer and star of the Blue Unit in which Greibling performed) let us leave the curtains open so we could see Otto do his pie act. I have one of his tin plates on the wall of my office and sometimes I take it down and hold it next to me. Everything he did, he did to give everyone a big hug."

To even be considered for the honor, a clown had to be employed with the circus for a minimum of 15 years, something that became increasingly difficult each year that another class graduated from this most unique college.

One Clown College graduate has been employed by Ringling ever since his graduation in 1971 but he has little hope of ever being named a master clown.

Tim Holst got off to a rocky start. When I first spoke

to him he asked if I wanted the "real story" or the one that was in the papers over the years.

Opting for the "real story," I learned that Holst was very nearly a Clown College dropout.

"They didn't like me,' he said. "But I came from a Mormon family in Utah and could not go home and tell my parents that I had failed out of Clown College.

Photo by Kim Cool

Ringling Bros. and Barnum & Bailey Circus vice president Tim Holst at a Blue Unit performance in Tampa during the debut of the 134th season of The Greatest Show on Earth in 2004.

instead I begged and promised that if I could finish the course, I would leave and never bother them (Clown College) again. As soon as graduation was over, I headed for home."

Back in Utah, Holst got a phone call.

"Where are you?" the caller said. "We were going to give you a contract."

He went right back to Venice. Holst worked as a clown for two years before auditioning for and winning the job of ringmaster of the Red Unit, one of the most important jobs in the circus.

The ringmaster keeps the show going, singing the major songs to introduce the big production numbers, announcing the acts and, most important of all, keeping things calm if there ever is any kind of emergency.

Eventually the man they "didn't like" worked his way up the ladder to become a Ringling vice president.

Logging more than a million miles in the air each year, Holst travels the world in search of new acts for the circus.

Only recently did he learn that he had two uncles who also were associated with the circus — as bill posters (advance men who traveled ahead of the show to post bills (advertising signs) to announce the impending arrival of a show).

Producer Kenneth Feld
Proudly Invites You To Attend
The Graduation Gala of
**RINGLING BROS. and BARNUM & BAILEY
CLOWN COLLEGE**

THE EIGHTEENTH ANNUAL
WORLD'S FUNNIEST FINAL EXAM

Saturday, November 16, 1985
7:30 PM
Winter Quarters - Circus Arena - Venice, Florida

Founded 1968 • by Irvin Feld

From the collection of Dixon Little

A coveted invitation to attend the Clown College graduation, billed as the "World's Funniest Final Exam," Nov.
16, 1985. The top graduates would likely be invited to join
The Greatest Show on Earth. Graduates of this Ringling
school were considered to be very employable in their
chosen field.

Circus Days in Sarasota & Venice

Like Smith, the trainmaster; Gebel-Williams, the famous animal trainer, fellow clowns Otto Greibling and Lou Jacobs, Holst was honored as a Circus Celebrity by the Ringling Museum of the Circus. His award, in 2004, was for being a Power Behind the Scenes.

"I learned circus by transfusion," Holst said. "I learned a lot from Charly Bauman. He had an eye for what was right. The devotion he had for his animals was something to see. I learned passion and hard work from Charlie Smith, who made sure I always had water."

(In the early days, every circus employee had a bucket of water a day for washing. Each performer's name was on his bucket.)

Holst's award was presented to him by Steve Smith, another member of the Class of 1971 at Clown College.

"That two more unlikely schlubs would lead such a life," Smith said. "Only in America could a little short guy from Zanesville, Ohio, wind up as director of Clown College. And only in American could a Mormon from Galesburg, Ill., wander into Venice and do so well."

Newer Venice resident, Dennis Hall, was in the class of 1972 at Clown College, landing a contract to tour with the Ringling show's Blue Unit in 1973.

"In the Blue Unit, we had Charly Bauman," he said. "He was classy but different than Gunther. In the Blue Unit, everybody had a piece of the spotlight.

"I thought I'd made a career," he said. "Alvin Bale was going to teach me the rocket."

Instead, he left the show after one year and headed back to Boston, where he ended up teaching clowning in an adult education program for seven years.

Photo courtesy of Dennis Hall
Dennis Hall as Dash the Clown. He was a graduate of Clown College, a performer in The Greatest Show on Earth and clown teacher for several years.

"I've done a ton of things," he said at the age of 55. "To this day I am trying to get back on the show. I'd still like to become a human projectile."

Hall has worked as a carpenter and as a house painter, skills he put to use even as a tramp clown, decorating his own Ringling train compartment to his taste.

As Clown College became more well-known, applications soared to more than 5,000 in a single year. From that number no more than 60 would be selected for the tuition-free program. Students paid their own living expenses and immersed themselves totally in clowning 24 hours a day, seven days a week. They had to be at least 17 years and they had to be U.S. citizens. Auditions were held in major cities throughout the country but some were accepted based on extensive written applications. Potential student clowns were "carefully evaluated for raw talent, motivation, flexibility and aptitude for hard work and improvisation."

Creativity was a must.

No sooner had Clown College graduated its first class than an edict was handed down from Feld.

" ...In 1969, all the clowns were informed that at the end of each two-year run, and the show would be revamped for another season, all the clown gags would be 'stored away' and all new gags would be used," Frosty Little said. "In those days we had between 25-35 clowns on each unit and used about 50 gags. I would get new gags from our 'gag' sessions, but never enough for the shows. We would get some more from the Clown College classes, but we still wouldn't have enough, so the producing clown would have to think up even more.

"Every time the clowns got a little spare time, in between the many hours of production rehearsals, we would be painting, building, sewing, etc.," Little continued "In addition carpenter George Shellenberger, painter Ivan Saxby and six additional sewing ladies were all assisting us to get the gags ready. At 6 p.m. on Clown Night, all the clowns came out in their 'Agent's Suits' (best costume). The circus owner, his assistant, the performance director and a few others people were seated behind a table. They would give the signal to begin. I would bring out one clown at a time. The clown would stand in front of the table to be critiqued on his costume and makeup. The critique was very tough, as it should be, since this was The Greatest Show on Earth."

After the critique session, Little would meet with the director of Clown College. While the clowns all went out to a chicken dinner at a Venice restaurant, Little and the director would meet with the president of the circus to discuss which gags would be kept for the show.

Photo courtesy of Frosty Little

Master Clown Frosty Little was associated with the Ringling Bros. and Barnum & Bailey Circus for more than 20 years.

159

Usually, about half would be accepted and the clowns would have to get back to work to find 25 more new gags. Just six days remained at that time before rehearsals would begin.

"During the six days we hade to develop new gags, build and paint the props, get the proper wardrobe and rehearse the gags," Little said. "This week was called Hell Week."

In the 1970s and 1980s, rehearsals began at 7 p.m. and ran until about 10 p.m., followed by meetings of department heads with the president of the circus, until nearly 1 a.m. Gags would be thrown out, and first thing in the morning the sewing ladies would be hard at work on new costumes for the new gags.

"Many times we would be painting right up to the time of the second dress rehearsal," Little said.

Because of the humidity in the Venice winter quarters from its proximity to the gulf, painters used a lot of Japan dryer agent in their paints to speed up drying time on new props.

Had they known what came with the coveted contract, would so many have applied to Clown College?

In 1983, a typical year, 45 students were selected from a pool of 5,289 applicants; seven were females. They ranged in age from 17 to 28, in weight from 80 to

200 pounds and in height from 3 feet 8 inches tall to 6
feet 6 inches tall. They came from 20 states. It was considered more difficult to get into Clown College than
medical school.

During the nine-week session, students learned

Photo by Kim Cool

**Lou Jacobs' famous car is part of the fascinating collection
of circus memorabilia on display at the John and Mable
Ringling Museum of the Circus in Sarasota. How a full-
grown man could possibly fit into such a tiny car mesmer-
ized and delighted circus audiences for years.**

make-up, designing their own clown face in the process; studied juggling, stiltwalking and gymnastics; and developed new gags they would use at graduation and later.

In several interviews given over his lengthy career, Little was quoted as saying that gags are "the essence of the art," further defining gags as "cartoons come to life." According to him, the best gags were based on real life but taken one step farther.

In an article that appeared in the *Venice Gondolier Sun's* Oct. 5, 1983 edition, Little described a gag about a mother being annoyed by her little boy. She buys him a balloon and he proceeds to break it. Then he hits her and she spanks him. That is the real-life situation that most people can relate to. This scenario became a gag when, in the circus ring, the little boy was hooked to a balloon, raised in the air and disappeared.

Faculty

Little and a cadre of other professional clowns, make-up and costume experts plus acting coaches, comprised the 30 or so faculty members of the college. Like any college there was a dean. There also were several visiting professors and guest lecturers.

Jacobs, considered a living legend in those days, was

Producer Kenneth Feld

Welcomes You To

THE EIGHTEENTH ANNUAL
WORLD'S FUNNIEST
FINAL EXAM

Saturday, November 16, 1985

7:30 PM

Circus Arena, Venice, Florida

THE GREATEST SHOW ON EARTH

RINGLING BROS AND BARNUM & BAILEY

CLOWN COLLEGE

Founded 1968 • by Irvin Feld

From the collection of Dixon Little

A program from the Clown College graduation, billed as the "World's Funniest Final Exam," Nov. 16, 1985.

one of the visiting professors, spending at least one day each term with the students, even when he was well into his 80s. It seemed fitting that Jacobs would end his career in Florida since he made his debut, at the age of 7, playing the hindquarters of an alligator. His brother was the front.

Jacobs came to the United States in 1923, joining the Ringling show two years later.

He is the creator of the circus' famous midget car act — one of the most popular gags in the history of clowning. He joined the Clown College faculty in 1974. Jacobs died in 1992. He was 89.

Another of the great clowns who taught at Clown College was Otto Greibling, a tramp clown who had extensive experience in some of the top circuses in the world, eventually joining the Ringling show in 1951.

Greibling stayed with Ringling right up until his death in 1972, teaching at Clown College during its early years.

Other faculty members included Florida Studio Theatre managing artistic director Richard Hopkins, who taught the art of improvisation, a skill possibly more important for clowns than for actors.

Consider that whenever an emergency of any kind occurs in the circus, it is the clowns that must improvise in order to calm the crowds, help them to escape if need be, or simply distract them for a time while some mishap is righted.

Another prominent Sarasota name involved in Clown College beginning in 1984 was the late Vicki Holden, who went on to become the chief costume designer of the Asolo Theatre Company in Sarasota. In her first year on the faculty of Clown College, she taught wig construction to the student clowns.

Curriculum

What's the big deal about taking a pie in the face or a broom across the back?

Timing.

Little himself ended up with four broken ribs in the late 1970s when he was hit at the wrong time and in the wrong place with a big board.

Timing is the essence of most things in the circus — from flying through the air with the greatest of ease to being propelled from a cannon or taking a pie thrown right at your bulbous clown nose.

There's even an art to spitting water.

Even after being accepted at Clown College, all the students did not make it to graduation.

According to the last dean of the famed school, some

Photo by Kim Cool

Jackie LeClaire served as the emcee of the Sarasota Circus Ring of Fame in 2004. He is seen in his business clothes on the facing page.

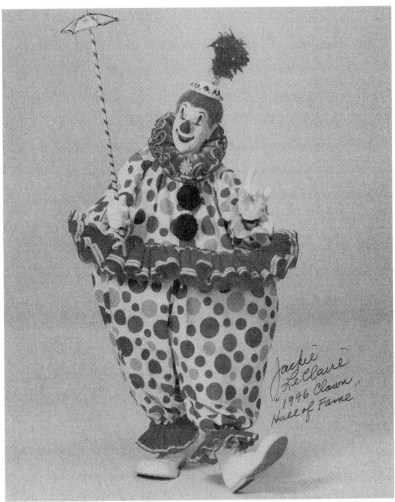

Photo courtesy of the Venice Archives and Area Historical Collection
Jackie LeClaire was inducted into the Clown Hall of
Fame in 1996. He is the only living clown inductee of the
Sarasota Circus Ring of Fame. He is the son of Ringling
clown Jack LeClerq. He was not a Clown College gradu-
ate but he did double as the aerialist Sebastian for Cornel
Wilde in the film, "The Greatest Show on Earth." He also
appeared as a clown in the film and starred in the
Ringling show in the 1950s and 1960s.

167

were not able to handle the rigors of this "boot camp" for clowns, where students were expected to absorb, in eight to 10 weeks, information gleaned by top clowns in careers spanning more than 40 years. To succeed, one had to be both a clown and a student.

Their teachers had become clowns in a far different way. Most had grown up in the circus, hanging around the dressing rooms, paying their dues until they were finally invited into the sacred area known as Clown Alley.

Budding clowns were taught the history of clowning, an occupation that dates to 2270 B.C., according to a Clown College publication of 1984.

A clown is "a divine spirit ... to rejoice and delight the heart" according to a 9-year-old Egyptian pharaoh who is said to have heralded the first recorded appearance of a clown in that year.

Clowning is said to exist in every known culture, especially in ancient Greece, where clowns provided comic relief for the Greek tragedies then in vogue.

Those early clowns became known as mimes and often performed with acrobats, tumblers and jugglers, skills that became an important part of the Clown College curriculum.

In the Middle Ages, clowns were called jesters but,

with their harlequin costumes and painted faces, they were carrying on an already ancient tradition. The term "clown" was not commonly used until the 16th century. It derived from "clods," a term that referred to country bumpkins, persons that were the brunt of these early clowns' humor.

In Italy, street clowns developed in the same era, giving birth to the *commedia dell'arte*, which translates into "comedy of professional actors. Harlequin, the most famous clown, derives from that era.

Only the Puritans did not like clowns, closing English theaters from 1642 to 1660 and even then banning clowns when the theaters were reopened.

Fortunately, the Puritan influence did not carry into Italy or into France where Pierrot, a white-faced clown, was popularized in the 17th and 18th centuries, about the time the first circus was created.

The first American whiteface clown, Dan Rice, began his circus career in 1840 and was thought to have been the model for "Uncle Sam."

But far more important than that, Rice is thought to have inspired five brothers named Ringling when Rice's circus played McGregor, Iowa, in 1870.

John Ringling, the same man who brought the circus to Sarasota, began his circus career as a clown, copying many of Rice's jokes.

On the other side of the Atlantic, yet another type of clown was being created, the clown auguste, a clown that wore eccentric clothes and generally played the part of the buffoon, wearing wigs backward and employing other zany gimmicks. This type of clown had a rosier face and very baggy clothes, which have endured to this day. That type of clown later evolved into character clowns, the most famous of which were Emmett Kelly and Otto Greibling.

Kelly was known for his Weary Willie character, who dressed in tatters. Greibling also dressed in rags but his character was said to be sassier and more crazed and eccentric than Kelly's character.

But for sheer staying power, no one has surpassed the extraordinary Lou Jacobs, who was employed by the Ringling show and/or Clown College from 1924 into the 1980s. Jacobs also is famous for being the only living person to ever have been immortalized on a U.S. postage stamp. His clown face with white-painted eyes that extended up onto his bald egg-shaped head, enormous up-turned mouth and rubberball nose was a variation on the auguste type of clown makeup. (*Jacobs' daughter Dolly carries on the family circus tradition today as both a clown and a founder of Circus Sarasota. Also an extraordinary aerialist, Jacobs starred in that capacity in the premier of the Robert de Warren ballet, "Ca d'Zan," at its world premier in Sarasota in December 2003.*)

All this history and more was crammed into the college's two-month program.

Student clowns studied the three basic categories of clown make-up: whiteface, auguste and character.

They learned to make wigs and rubberball noses.

They also learned to move. Choreography classes were held daily so the student clowns could learn to exaggerate their movements while still maintaining an intimacy with the audience. They learned techniques that would be useful in the Greatest Show's lavish production numbers. They worked with the circus choreographer Bill Bradley and others of his stature in creating their graduation performance.

To develop coordination, student clowns learned stiltwalking, progressing from 1- to 3- to as high as 12-foot stilts.

For slapstick routines, all student clowns studied gymnastics, learning to fall safely.

Other topics included unicycling, juggling, wire walking, improvisation, prop building, costume construction, magic, dance and even basic calisthenics. Students in the class of 1984 even learned basic puppetry and ventriloquism.

Considered as important as the curriculum was the thought process that student clowns would develop, something that would enrich their lives in a unique way whether or not they stayed in the profession they prepared for in Venice.

Instead of blue books, finals and graduation were all rolled into one really big show, an elaborate and hilarious extravaganza from which a chosen few would be invited into the hallowed tents of The Greatest Show on Earth.

The equivalent to achieving highest honors was to receive a three-year apprenticeship with The Greatest Show on Earth. These coveted awards would be given after graduation to very few members of the class. And even that was no guarantee of future stardom.

Of 35,000 clowns in the United States in 1983, only 300 were considered professionals. Competition for paying jobs in the field was tough.

Little is perhaps the most successful Clown College graduate, the only one to ever attain the Master Clown rating and the only Clown College graduate to become Boss Clown within just two years of graduation, a title he held for 12 years when he rose even higher in the Ringling ranks, becoming director of all the clowns in both the Red and Blue units of the circus. The only other Master Clowns to be named by Irvin Feld were Otto Greibling, Bobby Kay and Jacobs. Jacobs was Little's mentor. Those three were part of Feld's inspiration for starting Clown College because they were counted in that short list of clowns who remained in 1968.

Little himself went on to create more than 300 gags, was a full-time instructor at Clown College for many years and has even instructed clowns at the Japan Clown College.

After Clown College

Master Clown Frosty Little shared some information about Clown College graduates who worked the Ringling show for one or more years.

A few, including Keith Crary from Little's class of 1968, David Nicksay and Steve LaPorte went on to Hollywood. LaPorte earned an Academy Award for makeup in the film "Beetlejuice." Crary earned Emmy Awards for his work on the daytime soap opera "Days of Our Lives."

Billy Baker, eschewed Hollywood for Dollywood, Dolly Parton's theme park, worked on "Hee-Haw" and is building his own theater in Gatlinburg, Tenn.

Stiltwalking clown John Russell, after setting a record

on 31-foot stilts, moved back to Appleton, Wisc. where he makes furniture.

Peggy Williams, one of the people who nominated Charlie Smith for the Circus Ring of Fame, graduated from Clown College in 1970. After performing for more than a decade, she joined the show's publicity department before leaving to go out on the lecture circuit.

Chuck Sidlow, now living in Sarasota, was in the class of 1978 at Clown College. He too was in the show for about a decade, before moving to Japan for several years. After returning to Sarasota, he became the performance director and a performer for Circus Sarasota, a not-for-profit arts and entertainment organization founded by Pedro Reis and Dolly Jacobs. He is still performing as well as teaching.

George Shellenberger combined his circus background with his engineering skills to build props for the clowns for several years. He lives in Nokomis, Fla.

Clown College graduates Tom and Tammy Parish met and married on the show after being assigned to the Blue Unit where he replaced Little as Boss Clown in 1980 when Little was promoted.

More than one grad went on to work for McDonald's but none longer than Earl Chaney, who was Ronald McDonald for 18 years, after working on the

Ringling show for a few years and then in Las Vegas, where he now lives.

Little left the show in 1991 and moved to Burley, Idaho with his wife, Pat. He still teaches clowning — to "hometown clowns," doing seminars and workshops around the country.

Feld's decision to form Clown College was considered by circus fans to be the salvation of clowning in America.

According to college dean Ron Severini, a good clown has "a sense of the absurd. It's someone who has known comedy and tragedy and can still entertain the audience."

The logical next step was graduate school.

Graduate school for clowns

After 30 years of teaching the basics of clowning to an elite few chosen from hordes of applicants, Ringling Bros. and Barnum & Bailey folded yet another tent.

The last remnant of The Greatest Show on Earth was going to pull up its stakes in Venice.

The circus had left Venice in 1992 but Clown College remained for five more years. A victim of its own success, Clown College was said to have produced more than 1,400 clowns. Even The Greatest Show on Earth did not need that many clowns.

Times were changing yet again.

Ringling owner Irvin Feld had created Clown
College to fill a very real void. He died in 1984, a
decade before his son Kenneth would have to find a
solution to the opposite problem — a plethora of
clowns. The younger Feld's plan was to offer something
like a Masters Class in Clowning, open only to clowns
already in the business. Feld envisioned new specialized
routines, never seen before, that might grow from his
concept.

In January 1997, Clown College closed its Venice
doors. The following year, the first classes of a new graduate clowning program were held at the Sarasota Opera
House. Selected to head up the new program was Robert
Shields, who had had a prime-time CBS TV show and a
nightclub act that played the Las Vegas circuit.

Today's clowns, like David Larible, the first clown
ever named a featured performed in the Ringling show,
polish their acts inhouse for, as Larible's father once
said, "Clowning is the end of the process."

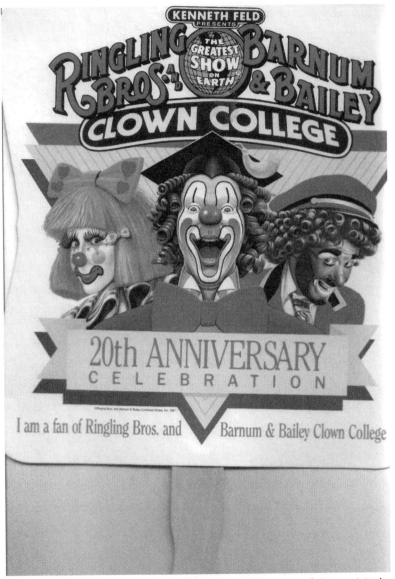

From the collection of Dixon Little

Circus fans needed fans to survive in the non-air-conditioned Circus Arena in Venice where Clown College graduation was held each fall after the 10-week course.

Kim Cool

Photo courtesy of the Venice Archives and Area Historical Collection
Clown College Class of 1986 gathers for orientation at the beginning of its session.

Class clowns converged at the 10-week tuition-free Ringling Bros. and Barnum & Bailey Clown College held each fall in Venice. A victim of its success, the school closed and left Venice following its 1997 graduation.

Feld reinvents the circus

Feld knew what he was doing. While the Ringling show was floundering, Feld had been paying his dues, preparing to fulfill his destiny as "The Greatest Showman on Earth."

He took a show that had been teetering on the edge of obsolescence and nurtured it back to health for the benefit of generations to come. Seeing the need for rejuvenation, Feld had the formula needed to revive it.

Clown College was just one aspect of his plan to put the circus back on its feet. Feld had big dreams and was tireless when it came to making his dreams come true. Never taking notes, he could watch a rehearsal and be able to critique even the smallest detail.

Honed in the early days of rock-and-roll, Feld knew all about the new arena venues. He also knew that they could be filled year round. Combining his entrepreneurial savvy with his experience as a rock-and-roll promoter, Feld soon had the show touring year-round and, as its owner, he transformed it into the lavish spectacle it is to this day.

Touring a show year-round for two years more than paid for the cost increases associated with the more lavish shows and the more spectacular acts he found on his annual trips to Europe and other places in search of the best and the finest. When he found the best, he did whatever it took to bring that act to America, even going so far as to purchase an entire circus in order to acquire Gunther Gebel-Williams.

When Gebel-Williams refused to leave the Williams Circus in Germany during the summer of 1968 because he worried about the careers of his fellow performers, Feld bought the entire show.

What seemed like a huge expense at the time paid off

handsomely as the man who became known for revolutionizing the treatment of circus animals became a household name and drew thousands of fans to the circus.

Gebel-Williams is said to have worked before more than 200 million people in some 12,000 performances, a circus record unlikely to be broken.

This was not the only time that Feld proved the soundness of the adage, "It takes money to make money."

But the best acts in the world would not fill the arenas without promotion and not since the days of P.T. Barnum had America seen such a promoter.

If people were staying home to watch television, he would give them something to watch and, at the same time, give them a reason to get out of their chairs and into the local arena.

Feld used television to promote his circus. In addition to hosting television specials, stars such as Gebel-Williams became frequent guests on major shows.

So did aerialist Tito Gaona, who appeared twice on the nationally syndicated Ed Sullivan Show.

And Master Clown Frosty Little. During his lengthy career with the circus, he appeared on 13 nationally televised TV specials with the likes of Barbara Mandrell,

Danny Kaye, Gene Kelly, Bill Cosby, Johnny Cash, Dick Van Dyke, Jack Cassidy, Lorne Green, Michael Landon and others.

Little said he was interviewed for TV more than 800 times. That was probably an understatement considering his years with the show and his stature as the last of the four Master Clowns.

National ad campaigns were launched. Some promoted the circus directly by announcing the show's pending arrival in a town. Other campaigns promoted the circus more subtly but just as successfully. The most well-known example of the latter is the famous American Express commercial in which Gebel-Williams walks into camera range with his beloved leopard, Kenny, draped around his shoulders. After that commercial aired, there was nary a person with a television set who did not know about the most famous animal trainer of all time and about the circus for which he worked. American Express got a lot of new customers but so did The Greatest Show on Earth.

Within three years as owner, Feld had made the renewed Ringling show so desirable that Mattell, the giant toy manufacturer, reportedly spent some $47 million to purchase the show.

But, after just three years of ownership, sawdust was

in his blood. By 1982, Feld bought the circus back, with his son as his partner.

Feld's secret to success was that he was both a sharp businessman and a flamboyant promoter. Slight in stature, he was big where it counted — in his leadership and business abilities — very much like an earlier showman — P.T. Barnum, founder of The Greatest Show on Earth, the nickname that stuck even after Barnum's circus was purchased by Ringling.

Feld also was part bean counter, running a tight ship. In an article written just after the showman's death, *Sarasota Herald Tribune* reporter Judy Huskey wrote that Feld had "made my life — and my colleagues' lives — miserable on many occasions. Controlling interviews, refusing to comment and making access to certain parts of the circus grounds impossible. I haven't always spoken kindly about Irvin Feld.

"But the five years I've covered the Ringling's activities for the *Herald Tribune*, have for me, personally, been a fascinating course in 'Circus Life 101.' I realized ... as I sat and stared at his now-darkened office window high above the silent arena floor, that Irvin Feld had been my teacher and I would miss him.

"I have come to realize that what he did, if not all of it, came from an unquenchable desire to do what he thought best for 'the CIRCUS.' If he and his family profited along the way, fine. The man was known for being a commercial wonder and the word is after all show business."

Ringling had profited from the circus and so had Sarasota. Because Feld profited from the circus, Venice did also..

Huskey continued her memories of Feld by talking about the nomadic life of circus people who live "a gypsy fantasy."

Continuing her written eulogy, Huskey noted that "He didn't have many personal friends in Venice and I suspect that might have bothered him. I also suspect it was the local people's loss. Ironically, or perhaps fittingly, he left this world in a town that is just now, perhaps, beginning to perceive what it had right in its own backyard."

Feld died in the Venice Hospital in 1984, and was succeeded in the management of the show by his son Kenneth, who had been trained at the father's side.

Like the latter-day Barnum he was, the senior Feld had worked his miracle. What Kenneth Feld inherited truly was The Greatest Show on Earth.

Primed to take up where his father had left off, Kenneth would not only uphold his legacy, he would expand it and perfect it in the tradition of his father, with the circus as the hub of what is today known as Feld Entertainment.

When the world calendar page flipped over into the 21st century, the Ringling Bros. and Barnum & Bailey Circus claimed in its circus program books that it then "became the only source of live family entertainment to have performed non-stop in three centuries."

Feld Entertainment's roots were in the circus but the branches spread from Hollywood to Las Vegas and Broadway, including deals with the Walt Disney Company. The Ringling organization even returned briefly to Sarasota, where it rehearsed and mounted Kaleidoscope, a one-ring circus, based on the very earliest shows but with a modern twist.

The one-ring circus, like its three-ring sibling, has not returned to Sarasota. It is following the money. Money has always greased the circus wheels one way or another. Although Kenneth is every bit the circus fan that his father was, he also is every bit the bean counter.

When the railroad tracks into Venice were in need of repairs that neither the railroad nor the city nor the circus could afford, Feld did what he had to do, he moved the circus.

When Clown College became so successful that

there was a plethora of clowns, the younger Feld did what he had to do — he closed its doors, but he also opened a new door when he created a kind of graduate school for clowns.

Bean counters always look at the bottom line. In both cases, the bottom line was the circus.

While Sarasotans and Venetians lament the departure of the circus and Clown College, the bottom line is that both cities profited from their presence and continue to do so.

You are cordially invited

to attend the Dress Rehearsal of

the World Premiere 108th Edition of

RINGLING BROS. AND BARNUM & BAILEY CIRCUS

at the Circus Arena, Venice, Florida

Wednesday, December 28, 1977, at 7:00 p.m.

It is requested that you be seated by 6:30 p.m.
(This invitation is not transferable.)

N⁰ 12 0

Courtesy of Dixon Little
A coveted invitation to dress rehearsal in Venice.

187

Photo by Kim Cool
At the John & Mable Ringling Museum of the Circus in Sarasota, a display of artifacts relating to animal training legend Gunther Gebel-Williams draws daily crowds.

Acknowledgments

This book was first suggested by Deborah Walk, curator of the John and Mable Ringling Museum of the Circus. Since timing is everything, especially when it comes to the circus, the idea had to percolate for two years before work began. During that time, while writing *Ghost Stories of Venice* and *Ghost Stories of Sarasota*, I amassed five notebooks filled with stories by and about people associated with the circus. They did not want to talk about ghosts but they did want to talk about the circus. Whether spirit-induced or not, this was a book that was crying to be written.

Information seemed to jump at me from a variety of sources. Soon I was on the edge of my seat, witnessing the spectacle of The Greatest Show on Earth from a very special ringside seat.

Help also came from friends and co-workers who have continued to lend their support in countless ways.

Thank you one and all.
Charles J. Adams III, Irv "Amtrak" Armbruster, Doug Bolduc, Roseanne and Baker Brown, Pat and Trevor Charnley, Antoinette Concello, Tina Gebel Delmoral, Richard Fischer, Beverly and Rilla Fleming, Tito Gaona, Sigrid Gebel, Kate Hadley, John Herriott, Tim Holst, Bob Horne, Pat Horwell, Dolly Jacobs, Larry Kellogg, Floyd Kruger, Jackie LeClair, Dixon Little, Frosty Little, Ron McCarty, Sue "Shammie" and Fred Menke, Bob and Melinda Mudge, Sarala Pinto, Pedro Reis, Charlie Schwartz, Debbie Shulman, Charlie and Kitty Smith, Angie Taylor, Jenny Wallenda, Deborah Walk, Jeanette Williams

Bibliography

Books

Buck, Pat Ringling; Corbino, Marcia; Dean, Kevin. *A History of Visual Art in Sarasota*. University Press of Florida, 2003

Gaona, Tito with Harry L. Graham, *Born to Fly: The Story of Tito Gaona*. Wild Rose Press, 1984

Gebel-Williams, Gunther. *Untamed: the Autobiography of the Circus's Greatest Animal Trainer*. William Morrow & Company Inc. 1991

Little, Glen "Frosty."*Circus Stories, Reminder Printing, 1996*

Matthew, Janet Snyder. *Venice, Journey From Horse and Chaise, a History of Venice, Florida*. Pine Level Press Inc. 1989

O'Nan, Stewart, *The Circus Fire, A True Story of An American Tragedy*, Anchor Books, a Division of Random House. 2000

Sulzer, Elmer G. *Ghost Railroads of Sarasota County*, Sarasota County Historical Commission, 1971

Periodicals

Banner Line

Sarasota Herald Tribune

Sarasota Historical Society Newsletters and archives

Sarasota News

Venice Archives and Area Historical Collection

Venice Gondolier Sun

About the author

Seated on an historic bench
at Animal Kingdom Lodge

Kim Cool has written business, needlecraft, travel and ghost story books. In the works are *Ghost Stories of Tampa* and *Ghost Stories of Clearwater/St. Petersburg.* Also on the horizon is *Circus Folks of Sarasota and Venice, Where Are They Now?* a sequel to *Circus Days in Sarasota and Venice.*

By day, the Sweet Briar College graduate writes about Venice, entertainment, homes and travel as the Features Editor of the *Venice Gondolier Sun.* She is a member of the Circus Historical Society, Historical Society of Sarasota County, Venice Archives and Area Historical Collection, the Venice Historical Society, the Advisory Board of the Salvation Army, a national synchronized, senior competition and gold test judge for the United States Figure Skating Association, a former competitive curler at the national level and a charter member of the Florida Curling Club.

The writer has won awards from the Florida Press Association for articles about the environment, religion and travel.

She is listed in Who's Who of American Women, Who's Who in the South and Southwest and other reference works.

In her spare time she is likely to be found at Walt Disney World, stalking Donald (the Duck).

Afterword

The Greatest Show on Earth left a legacy in both Sarasota and Venice. It is visible in everything from street names to the cultural climate of the area.

Less visible, but possibly more important is the character of the people who dwell in Sarasota County. Many have a connection to The Ringling Bros. and Barnum & Bailey Circus, to other circuses that have wintered or continue to winter in the area, or, like Mayor Louann Palmer of Sarasota, a connection to Sarasota High School's famous Sailor Circus. Many were drawn to the area when the circus was here.

Because they came and because they stayed, Sarasota and Venice will always be known as Circus Cities, and will be just a bit more special.

That is my story and I am sticking to it.

You may contact me via e-mail at:
kimcool@historicvenicepress.com

or by regular mail to Kim Cool at:
Historic Venice Press
PO Box 800
Venice, FL 34285

Kim Cool

Venice, Florida

April 2004

HISTORIC VENICE PRESS
ORDER FORM

Circus Days in Sarasota and Venice..........................$18.95
     ISBN 0-9721655-3-3

Ghost Stories of Sarasota..$12.95
     ISBN 0-9721655-1-7

Ghost Stories of Venice..$8.95
     ISBN 0-9721655-0-9

Indicate the number of books you wish to order below:

No. ordered

_____	Circus Days @ 18.95	_____
_____	Sarasota @ 12.95	_____
_____	Venice @ 8.95	_____

_____   Sub total   _____

Florida residents add 7 percent sales tax   _____

Shipping to one address $3.50

TOTAL AMOUNT ENCLOSED: _____

MAIL TO:

Historic Venice Press
PO Box 800
Venice, FL 34285

In 1960, the Venice Gondolier Sun conducted a survey to see if the average citizen was as positive about the impact the circus was likely to have on Venice. More than 30 years later the same paper would conduct a similar survey before the circus pulled out of Venice. The results of both surveys were virtually the same — an overwhelming majority of readers liked the circus and were happy to have it in town.